This book belongs to

little princess

Name:

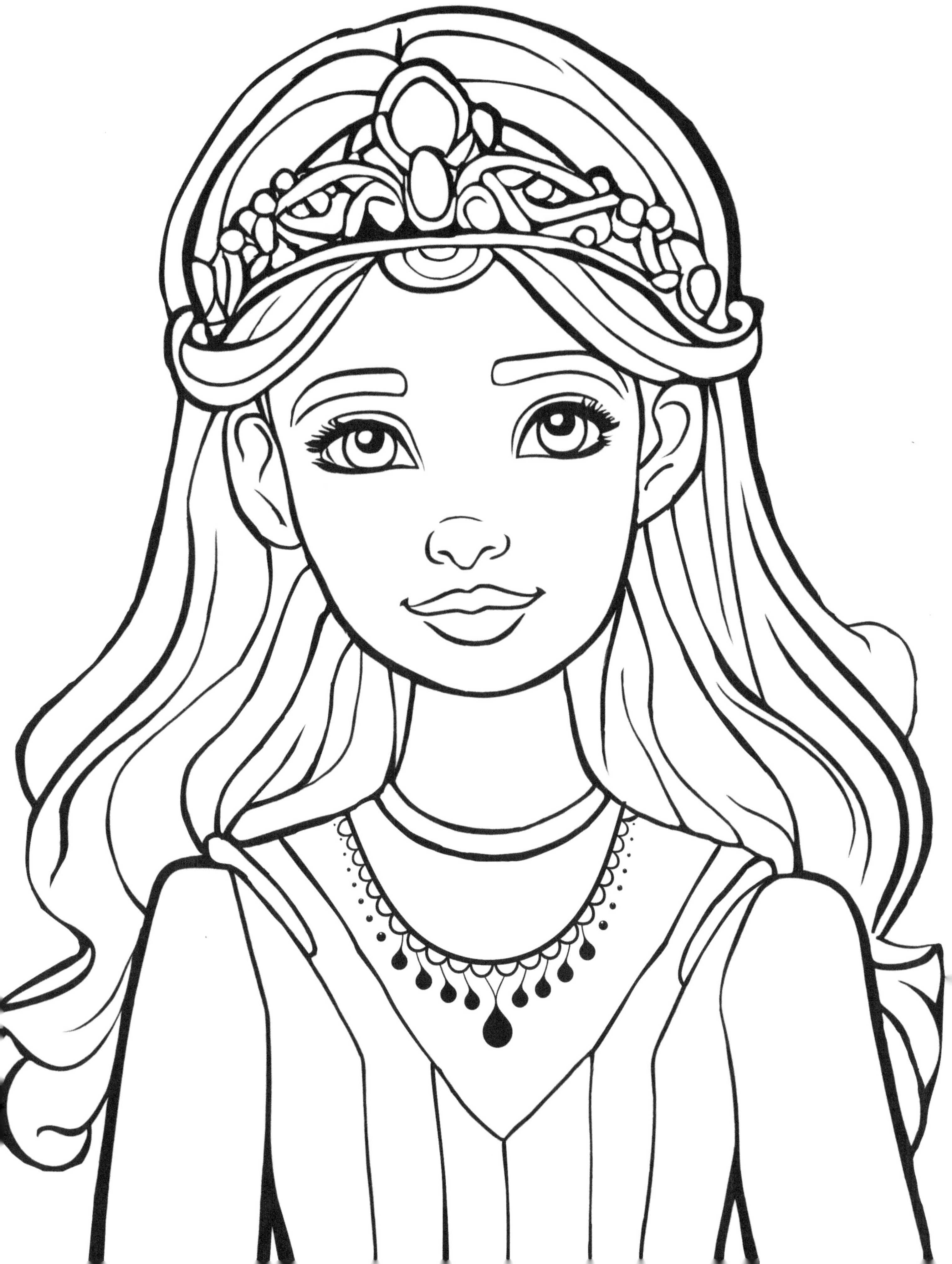

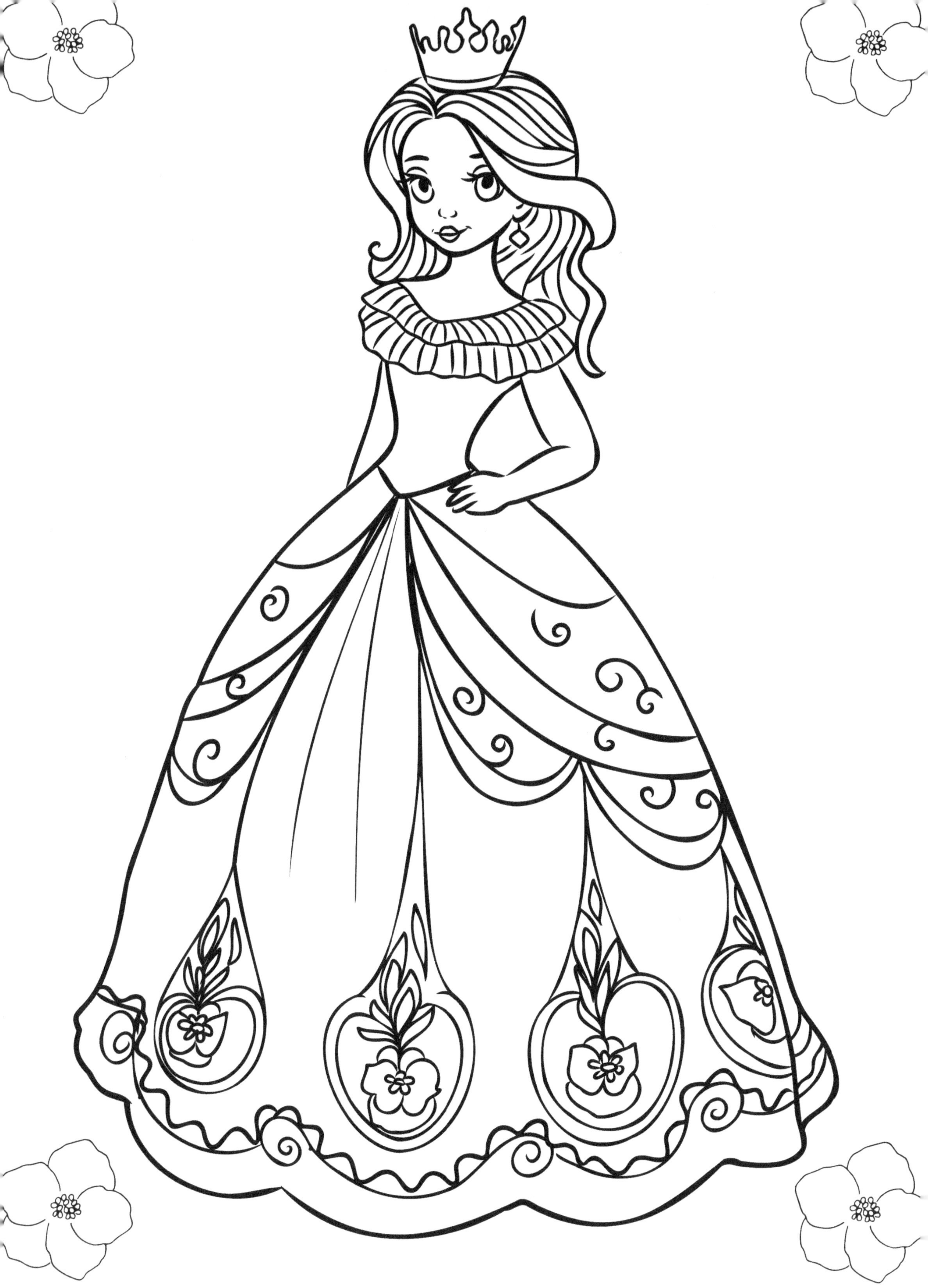

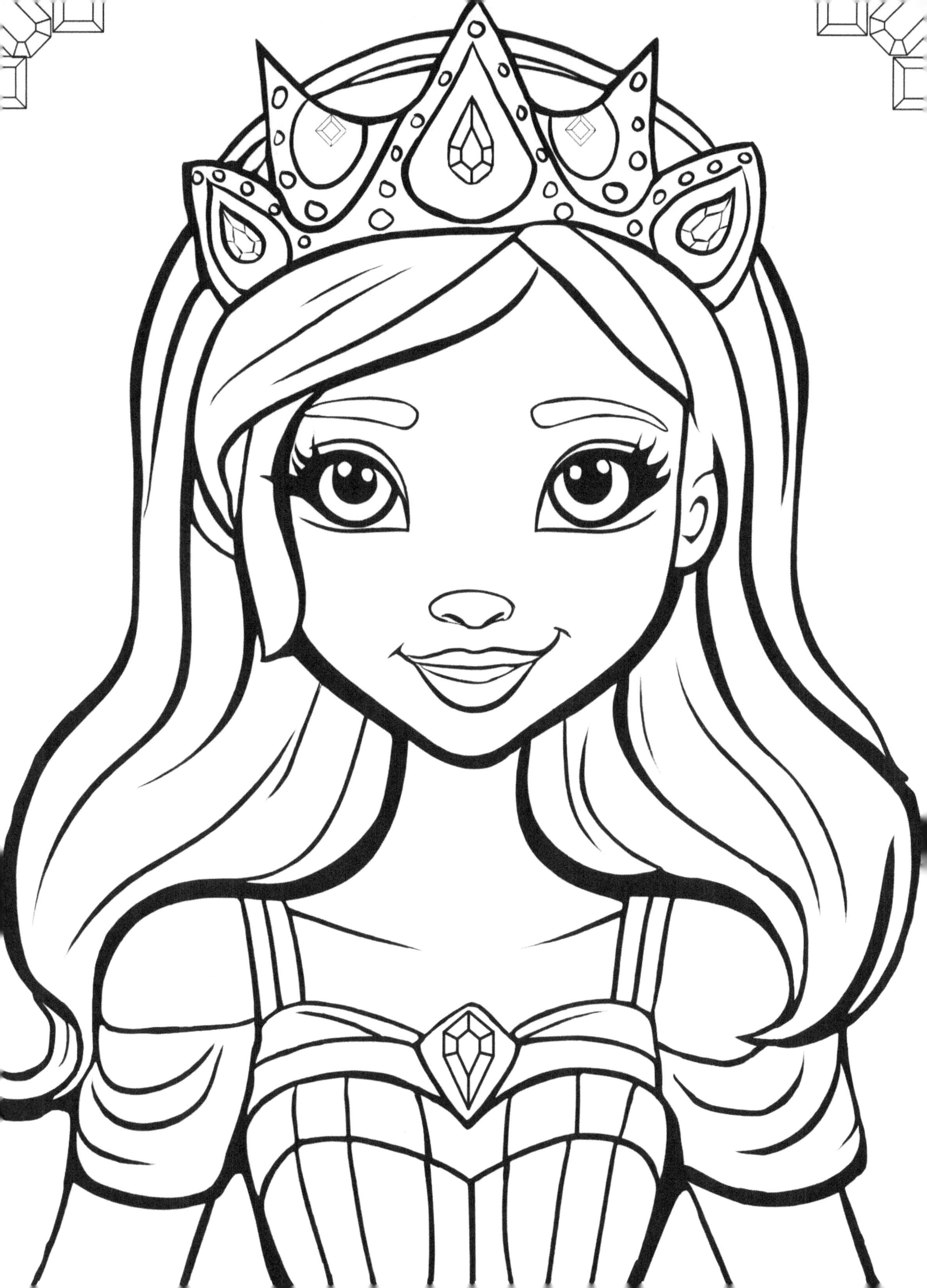

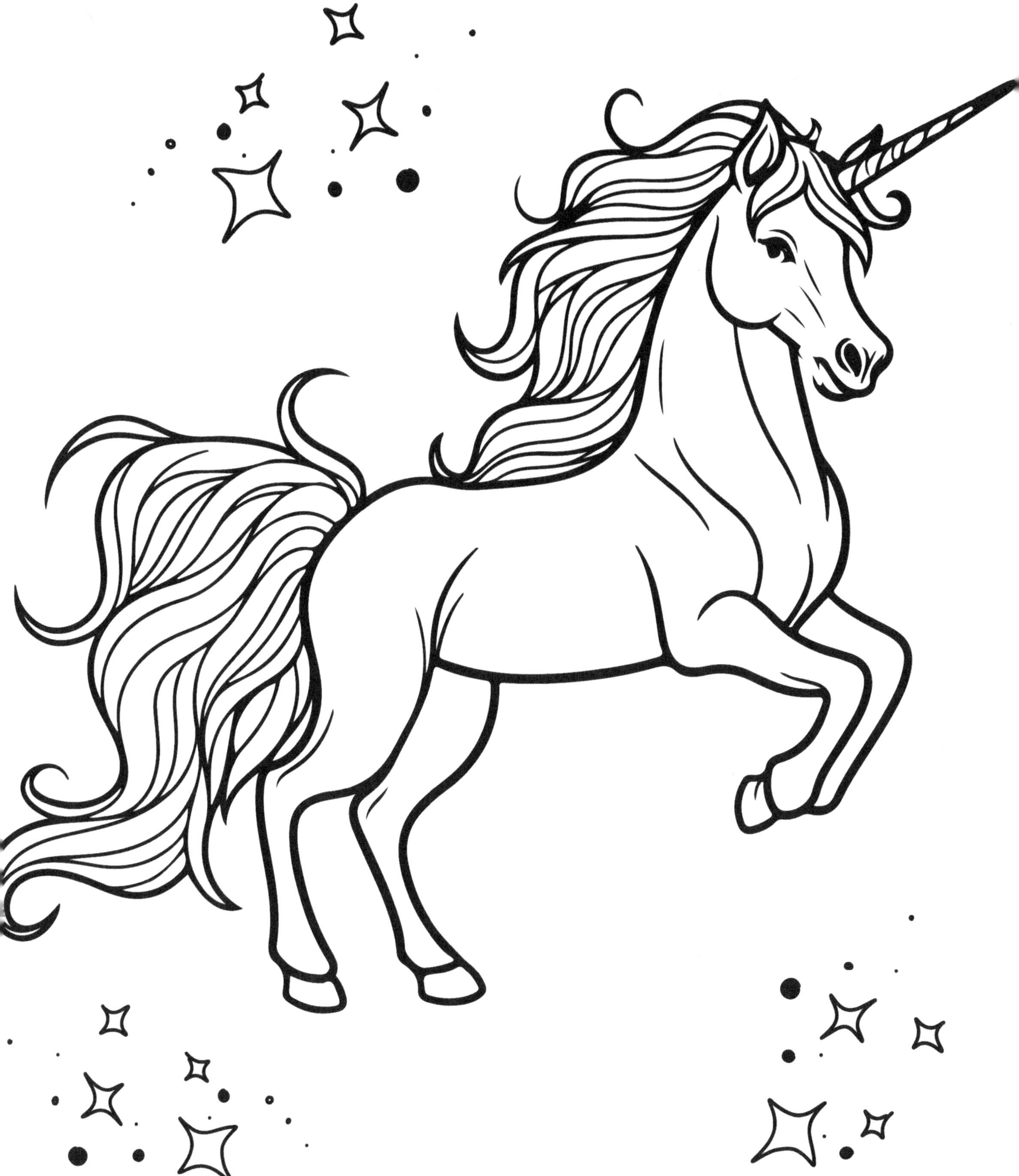

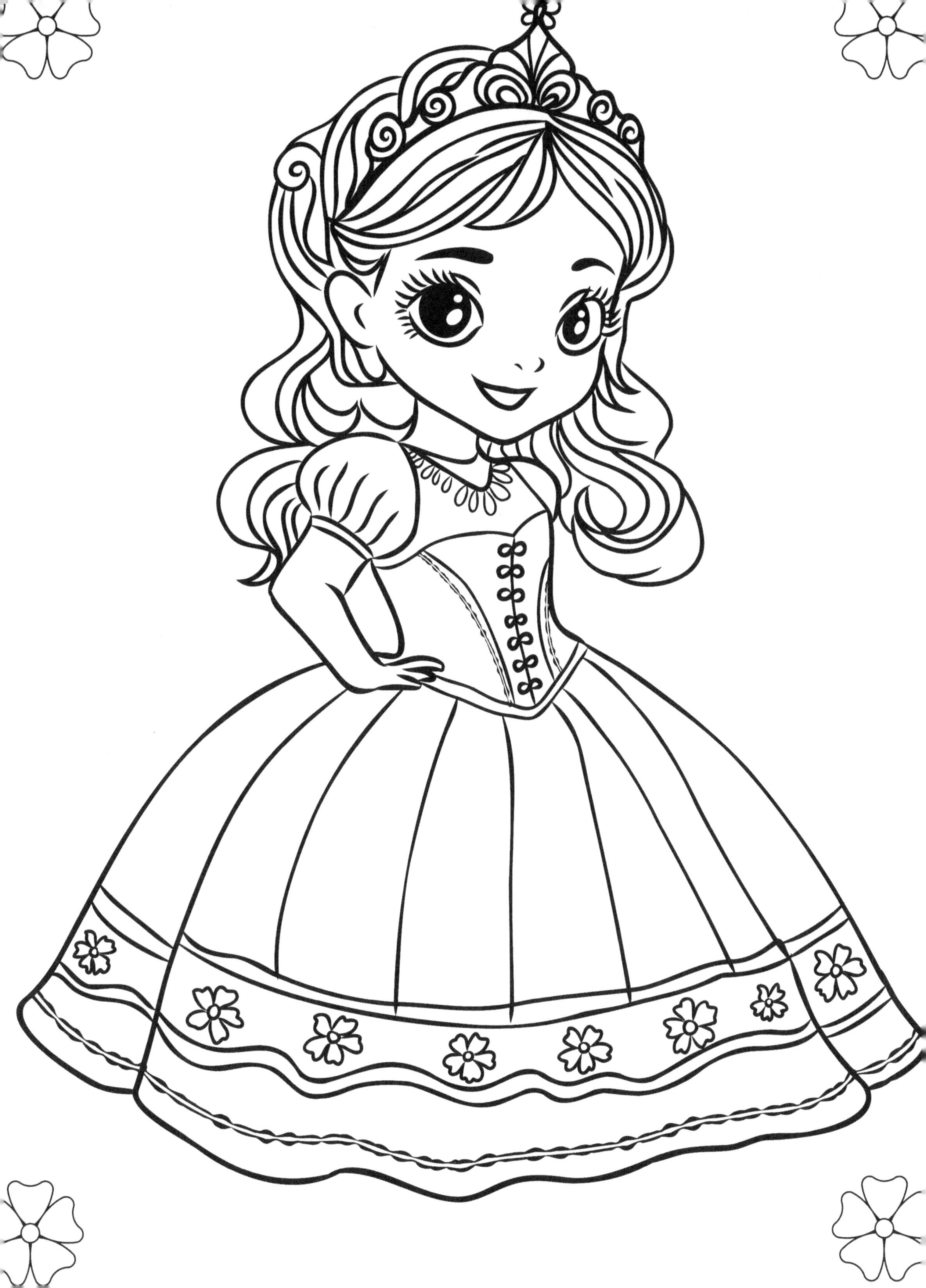

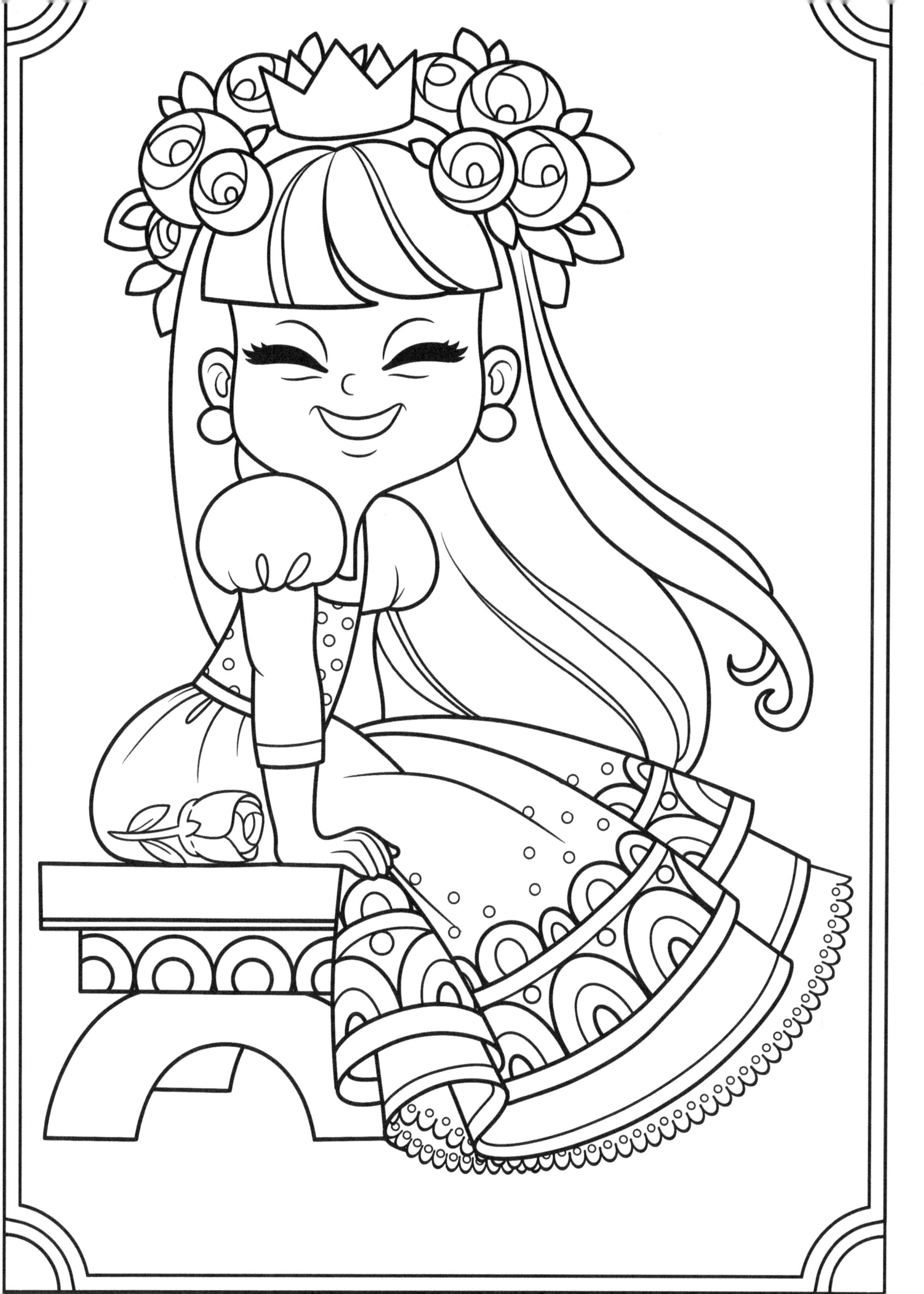

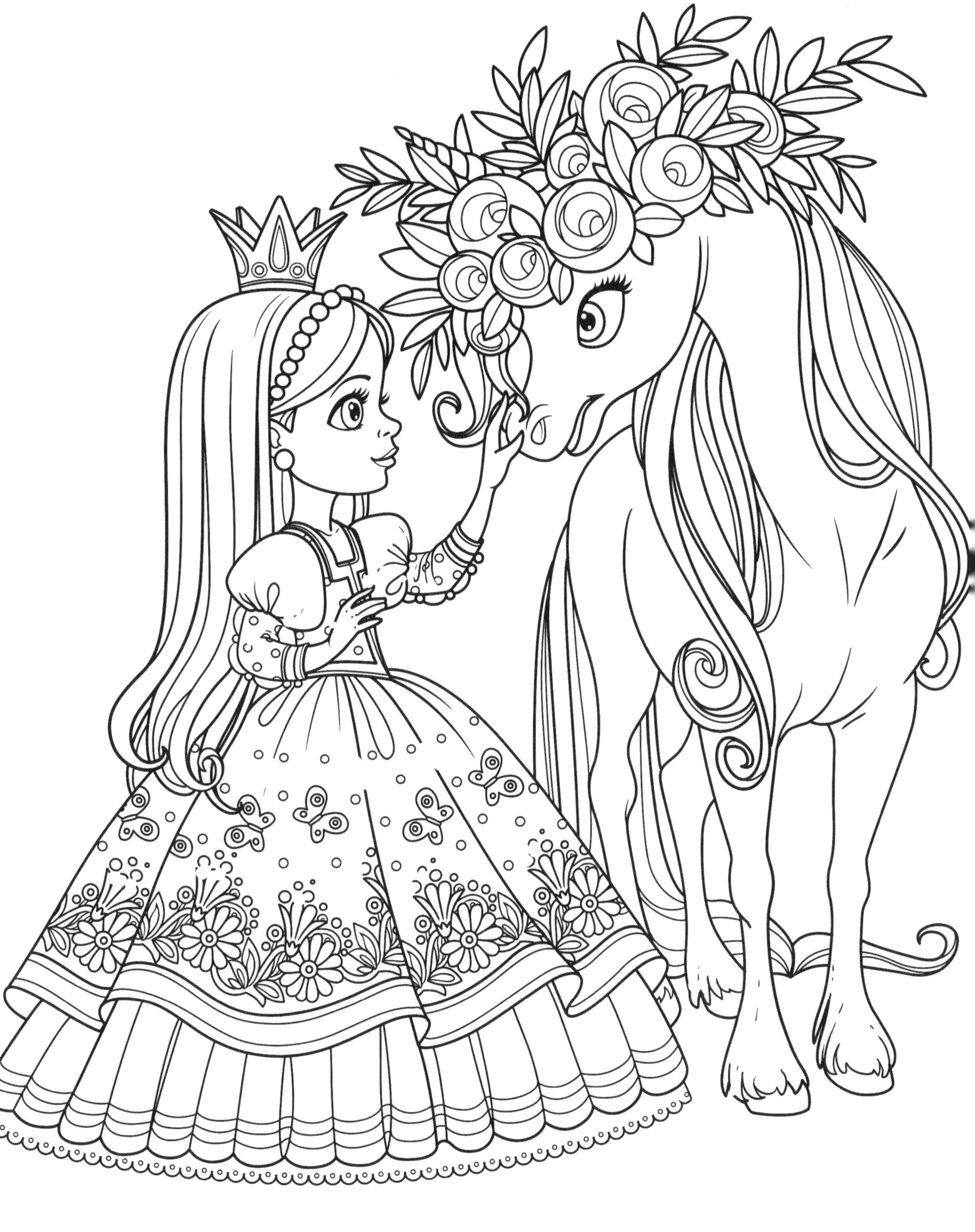

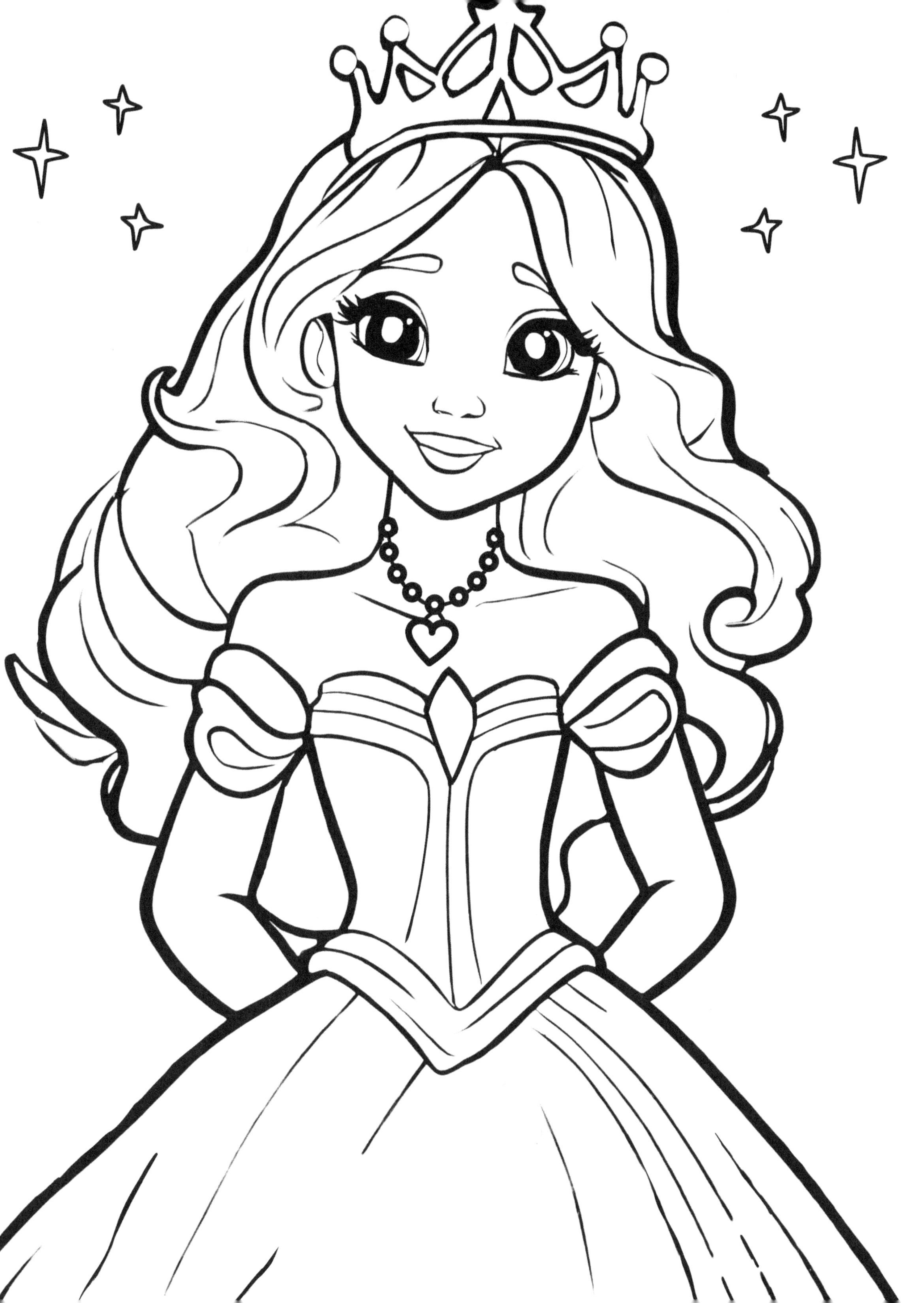

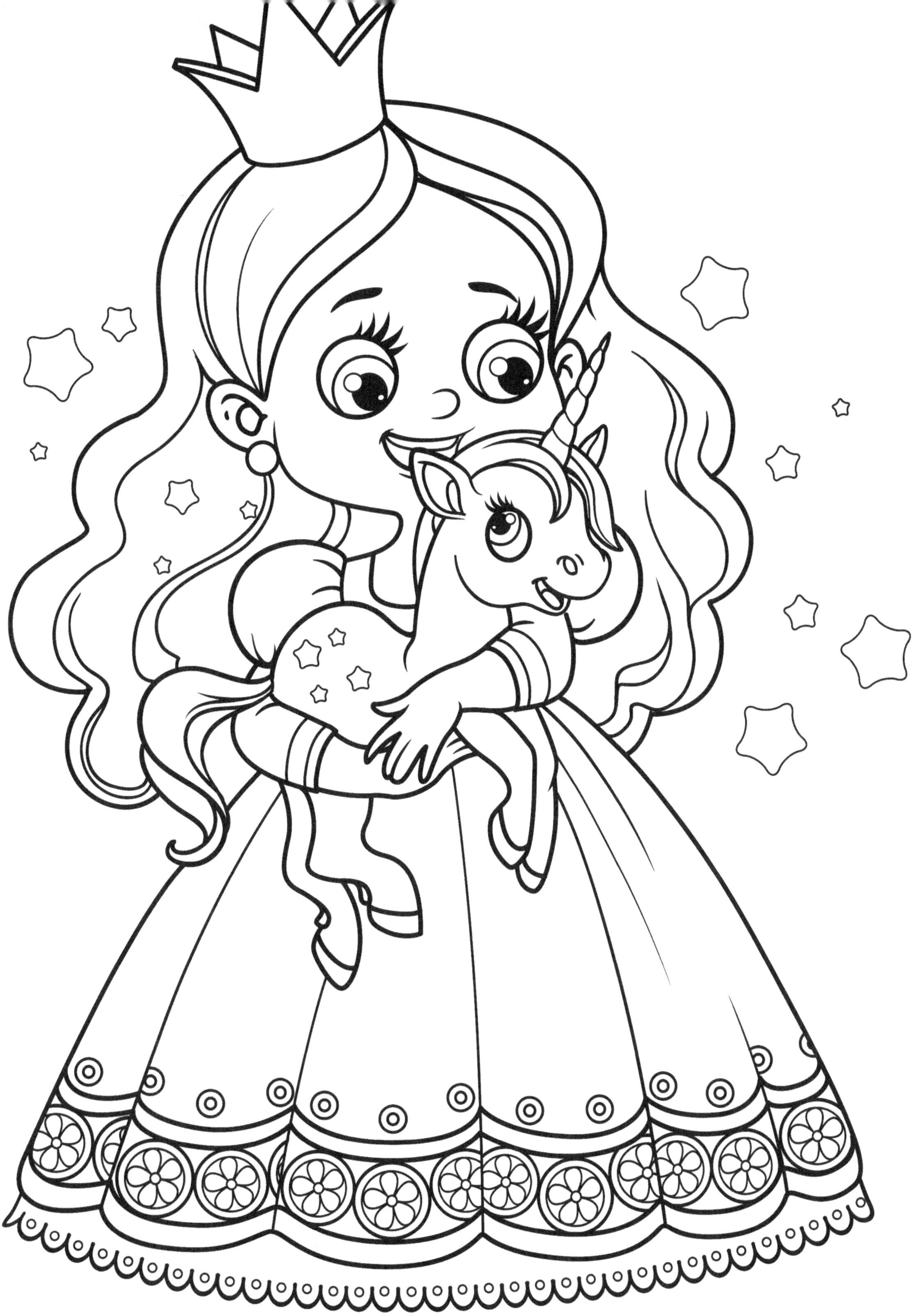

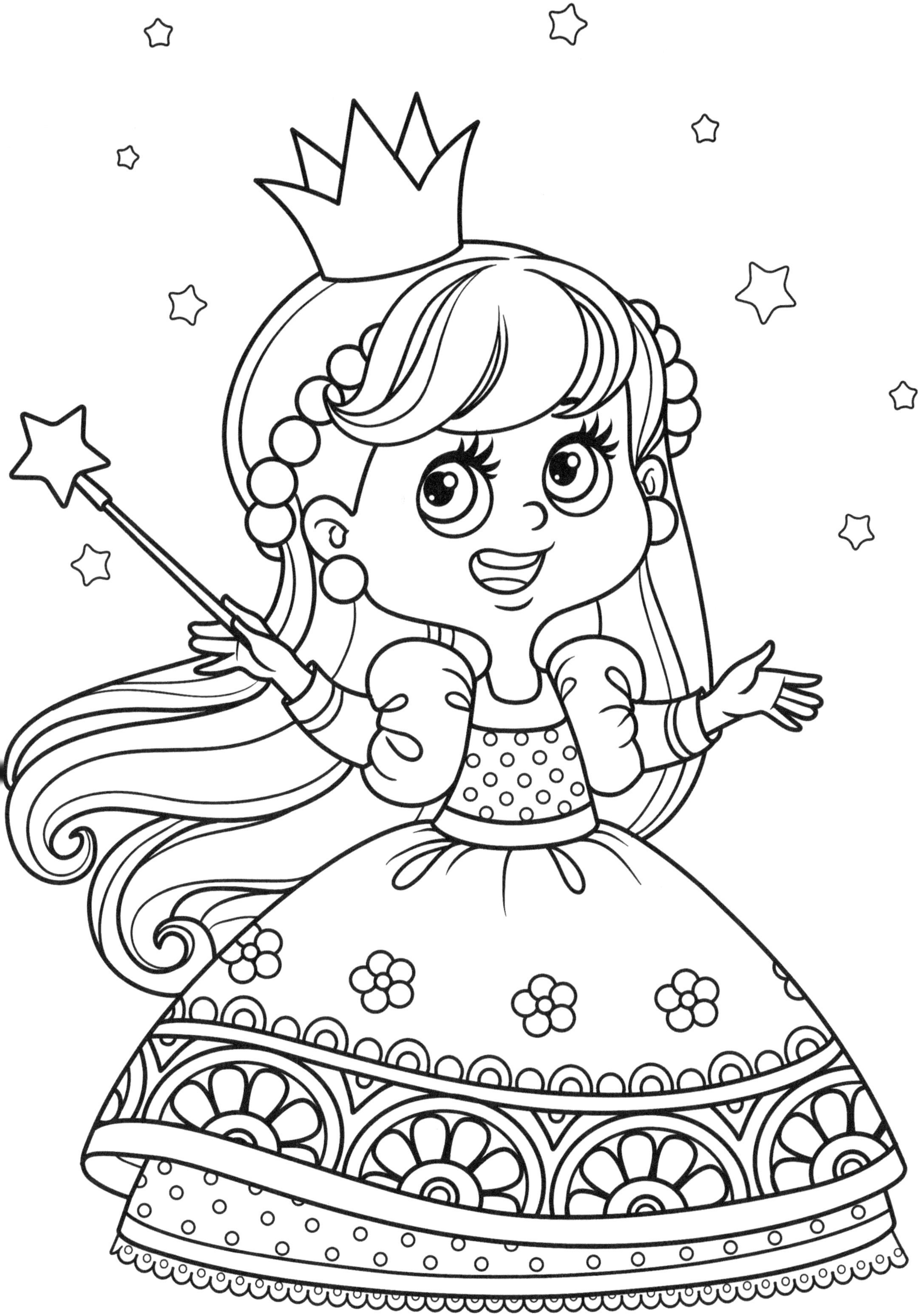

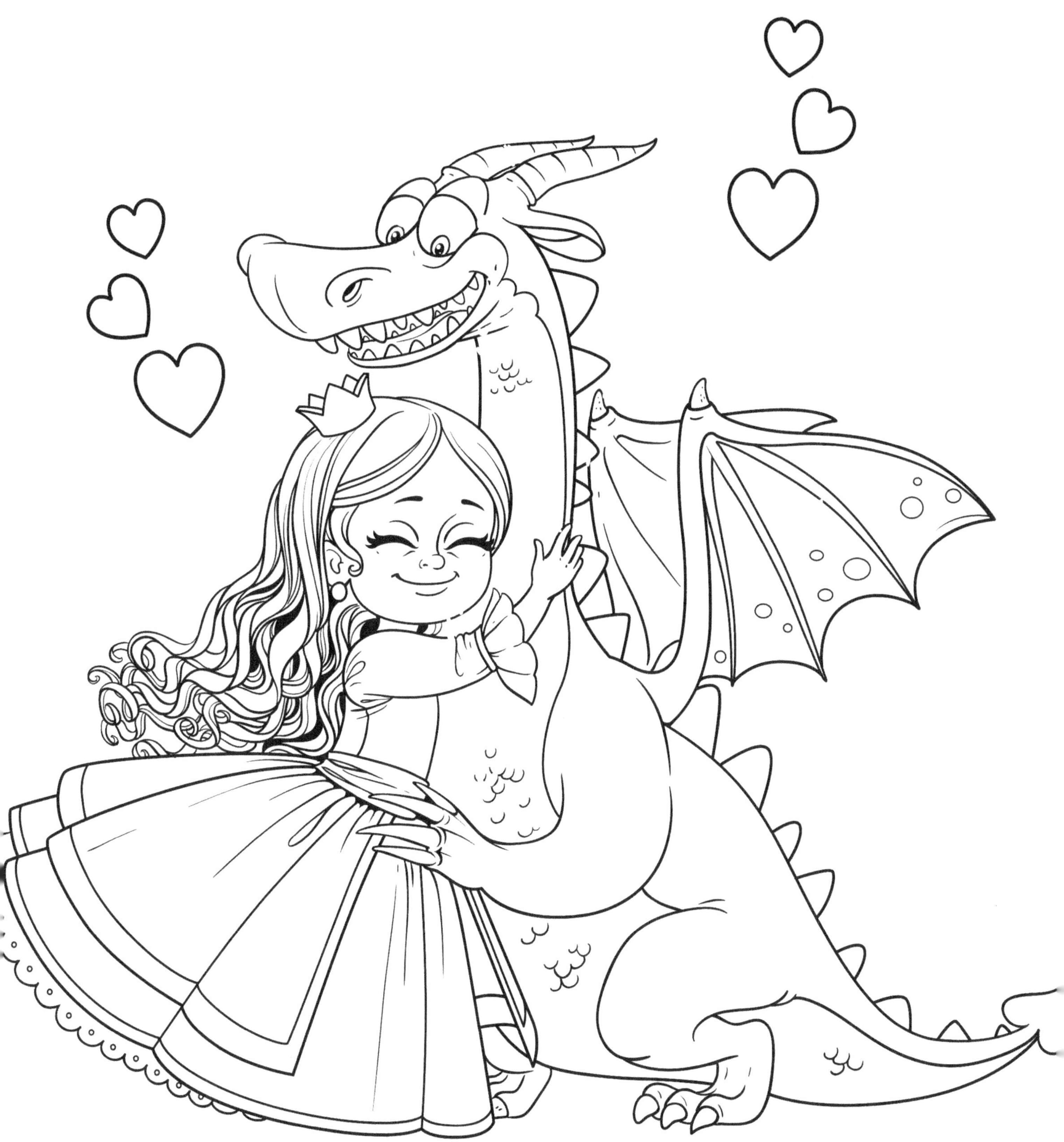

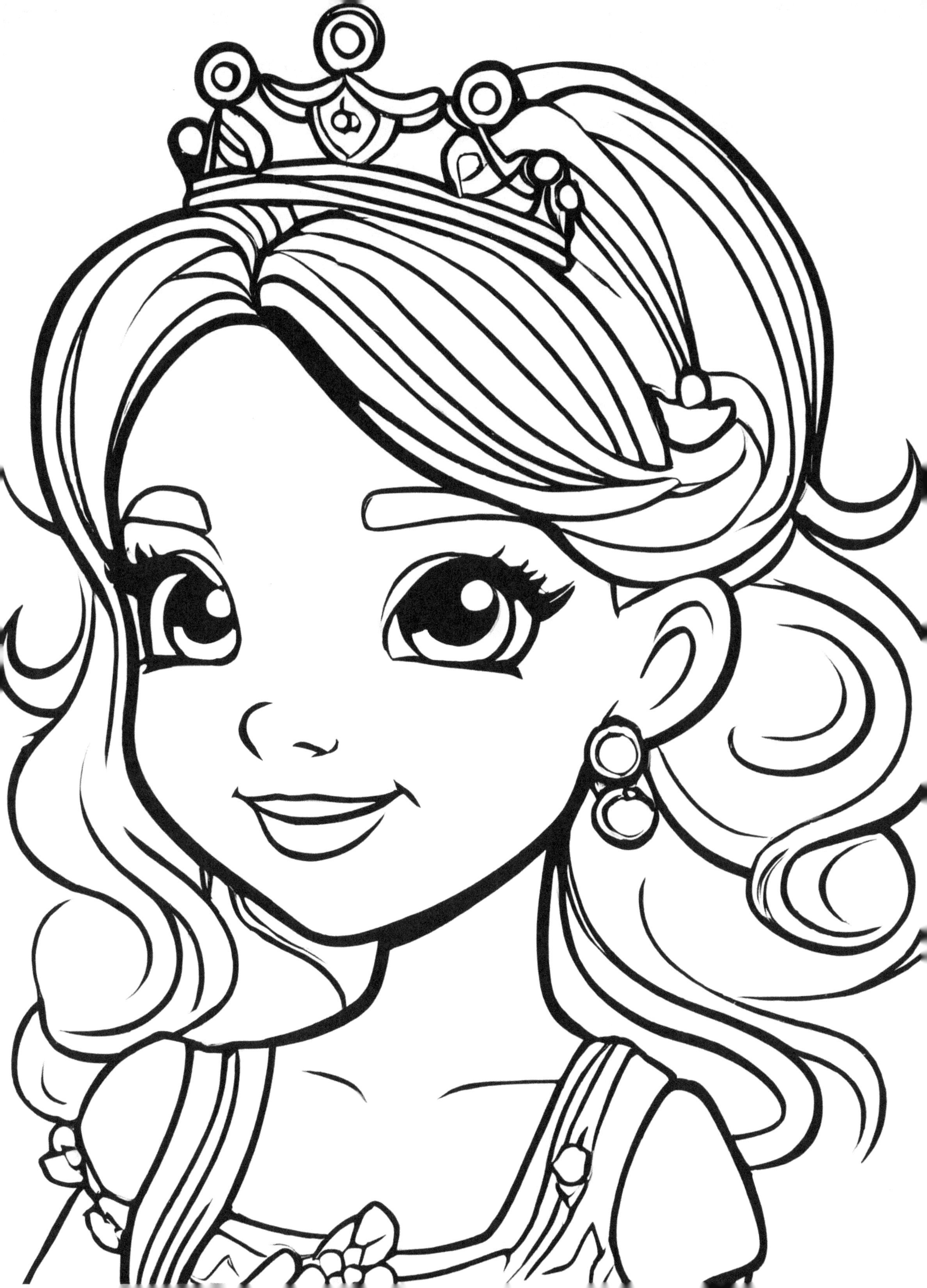

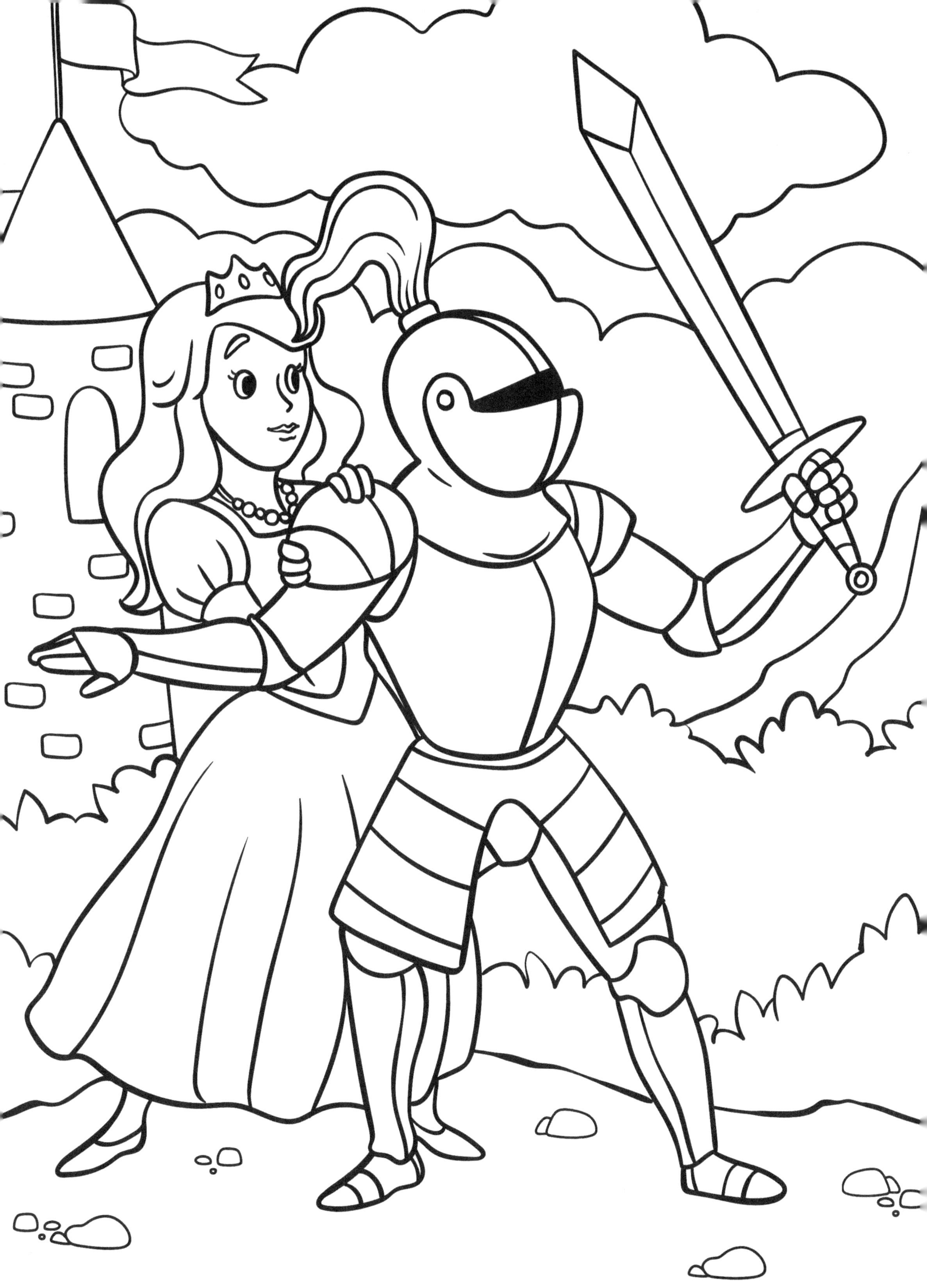

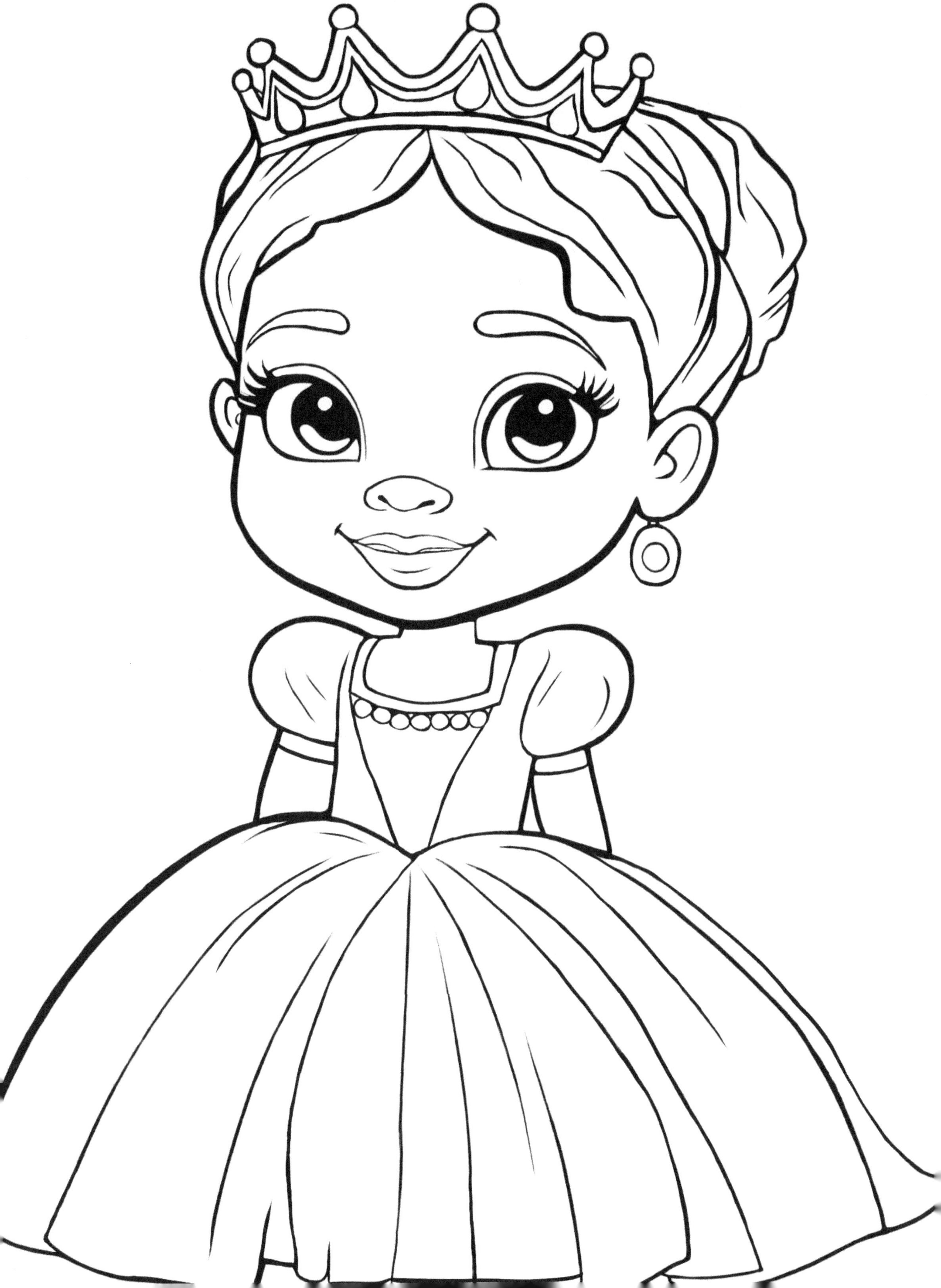

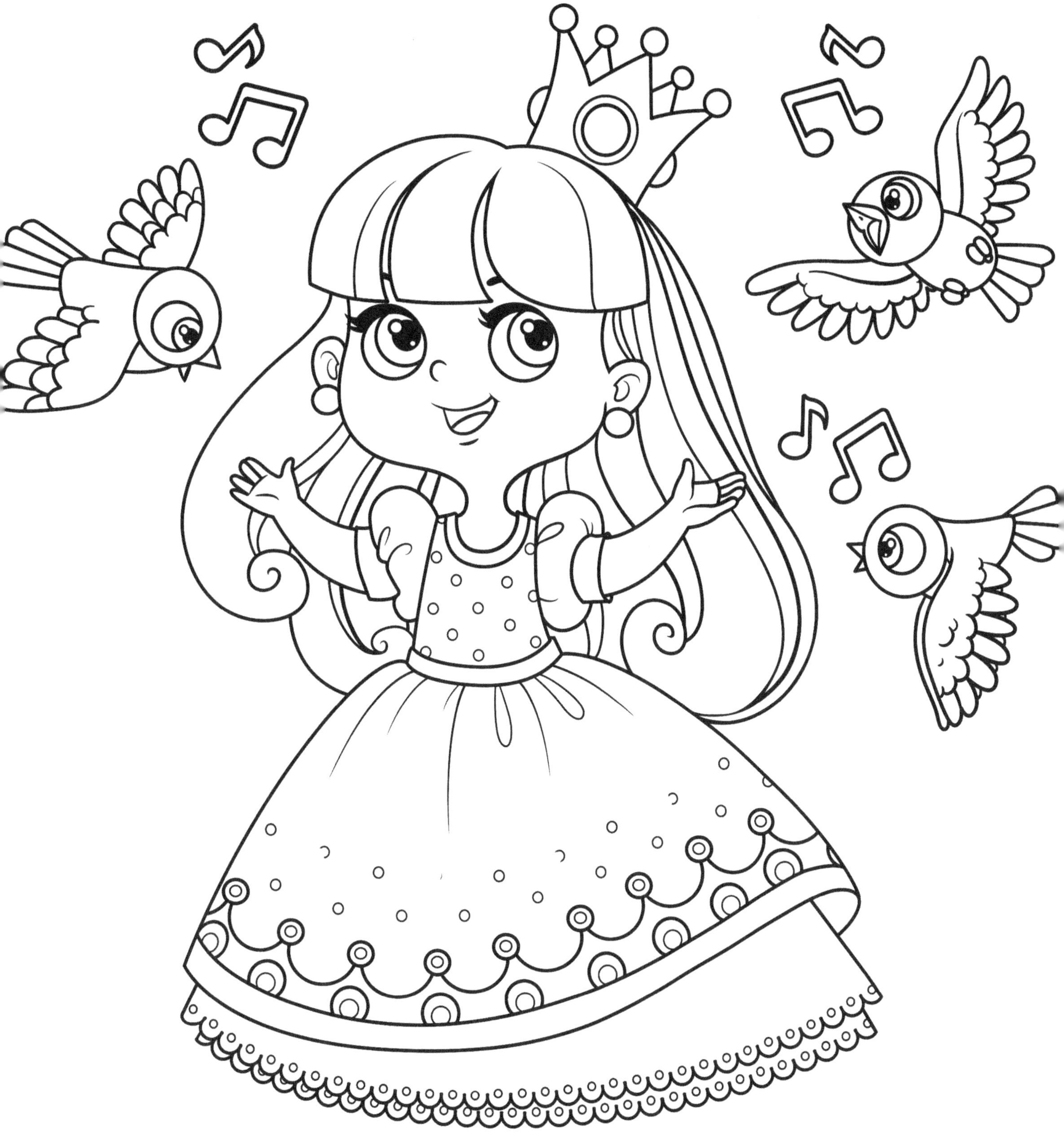

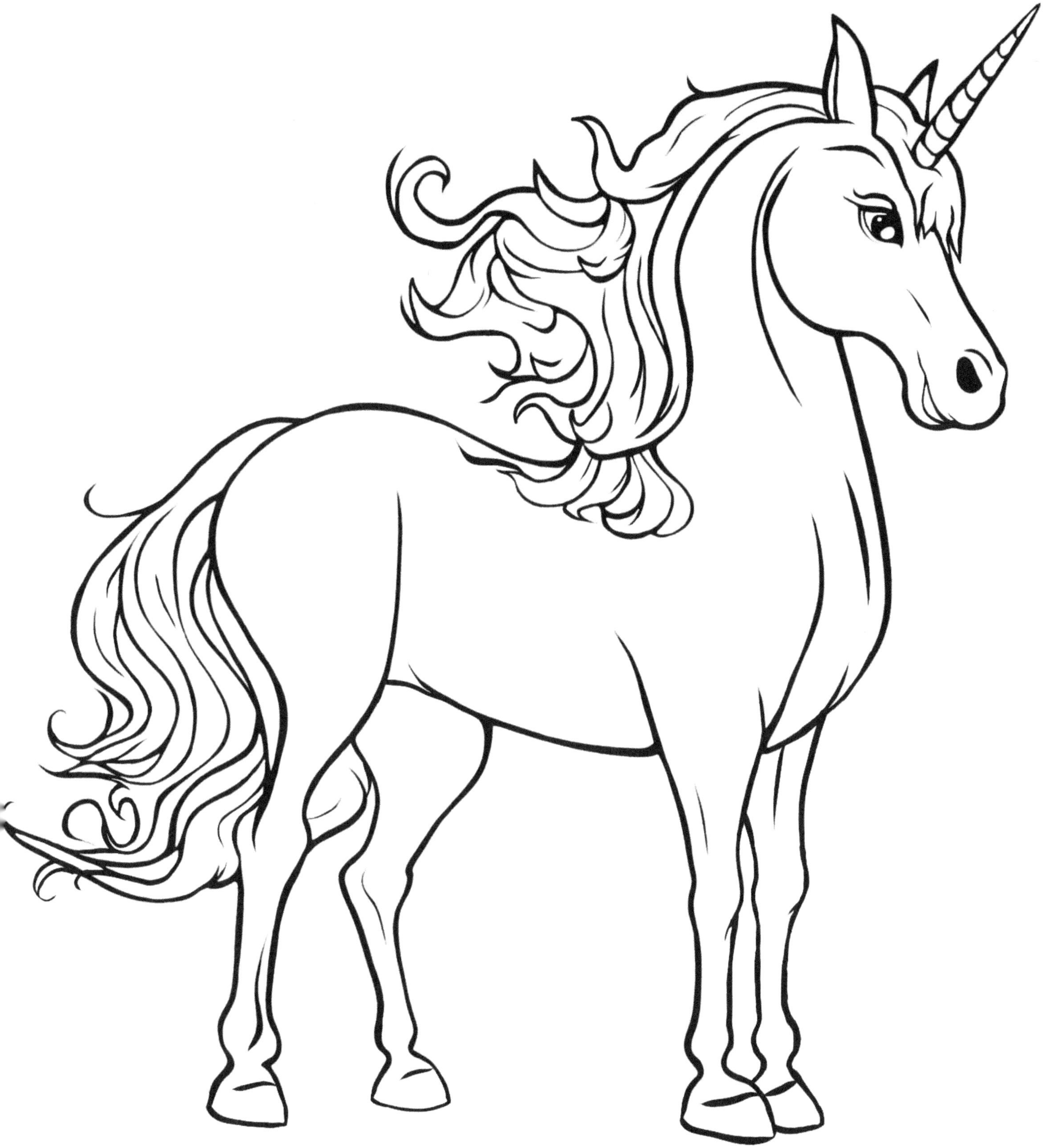

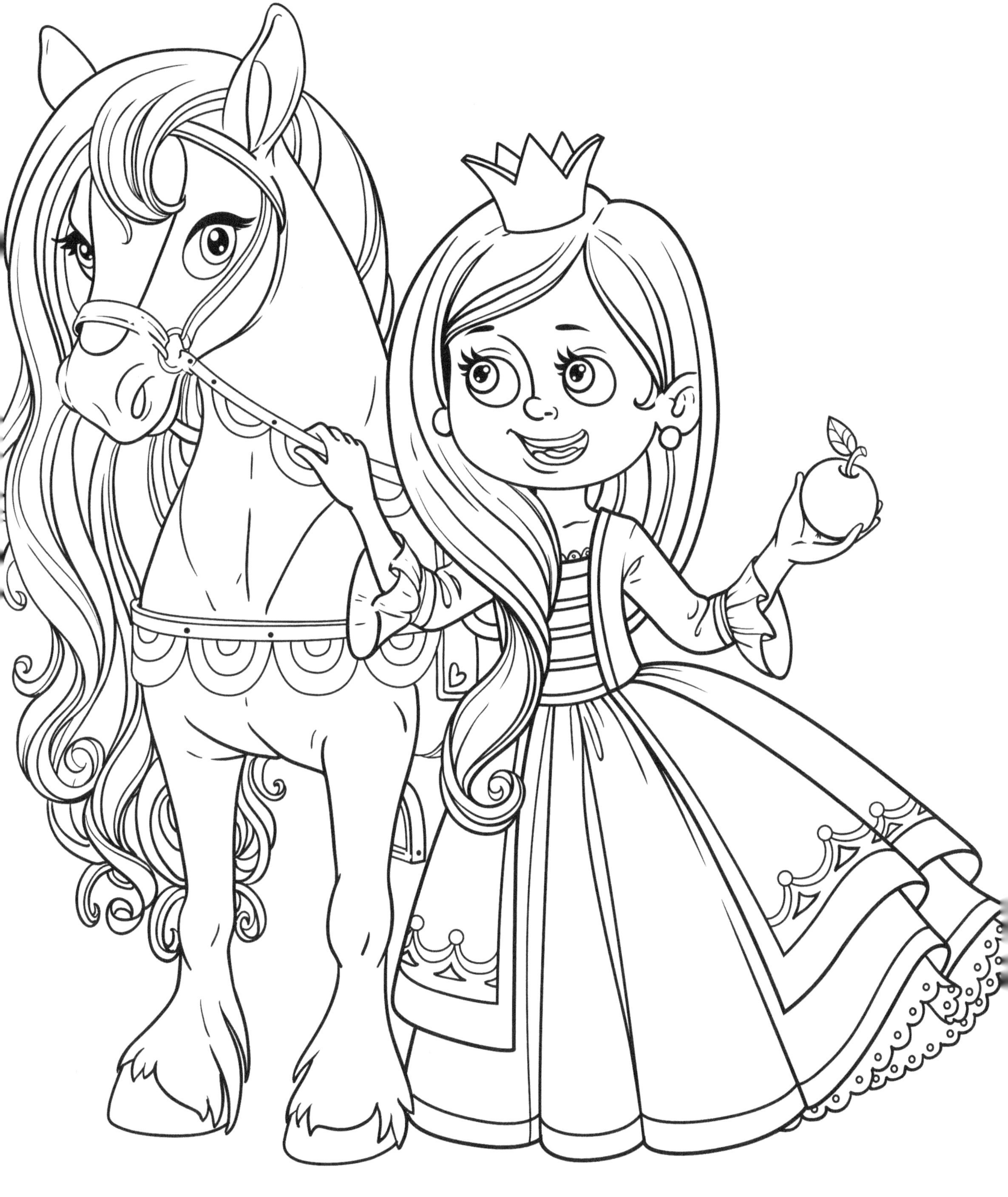

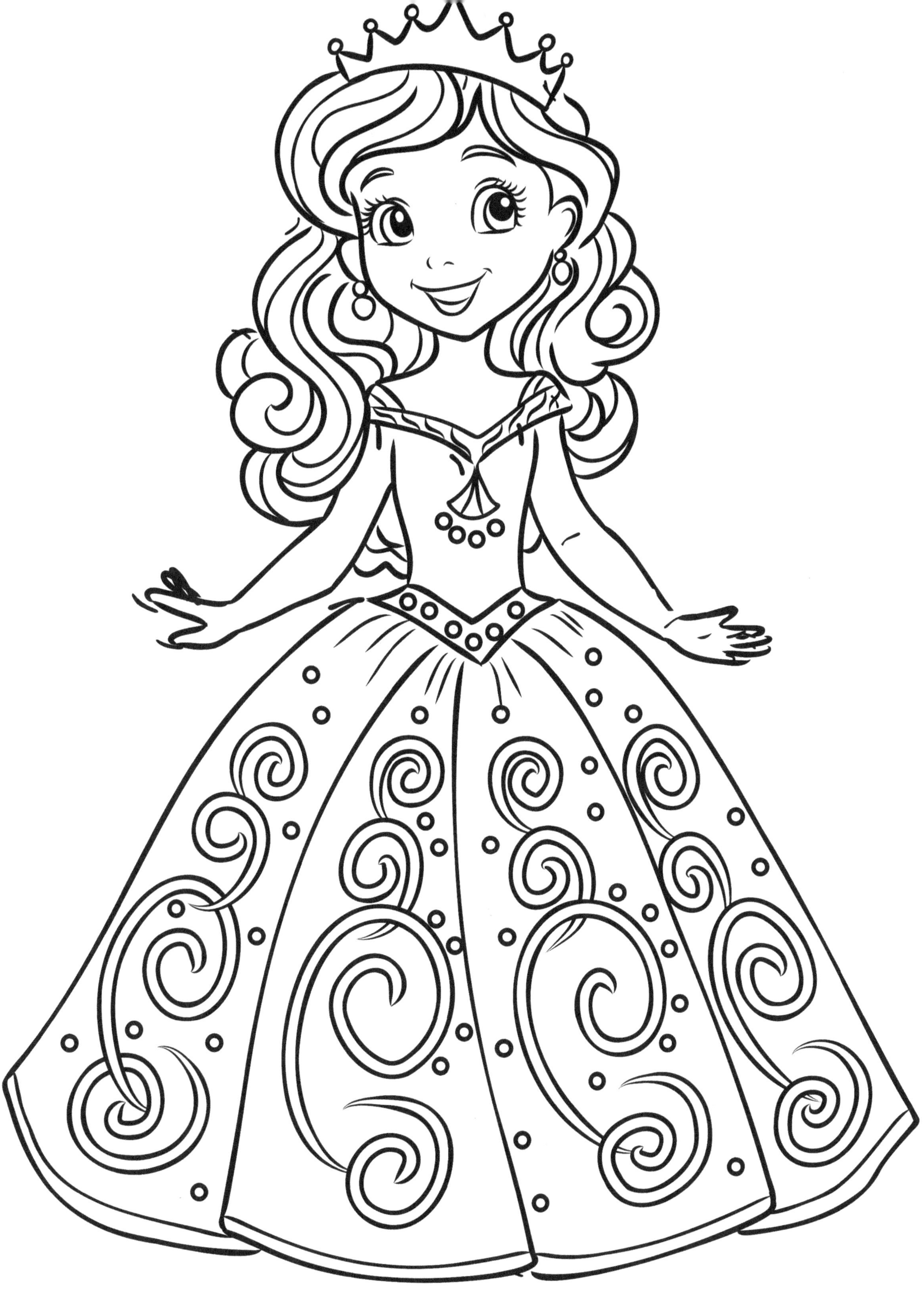

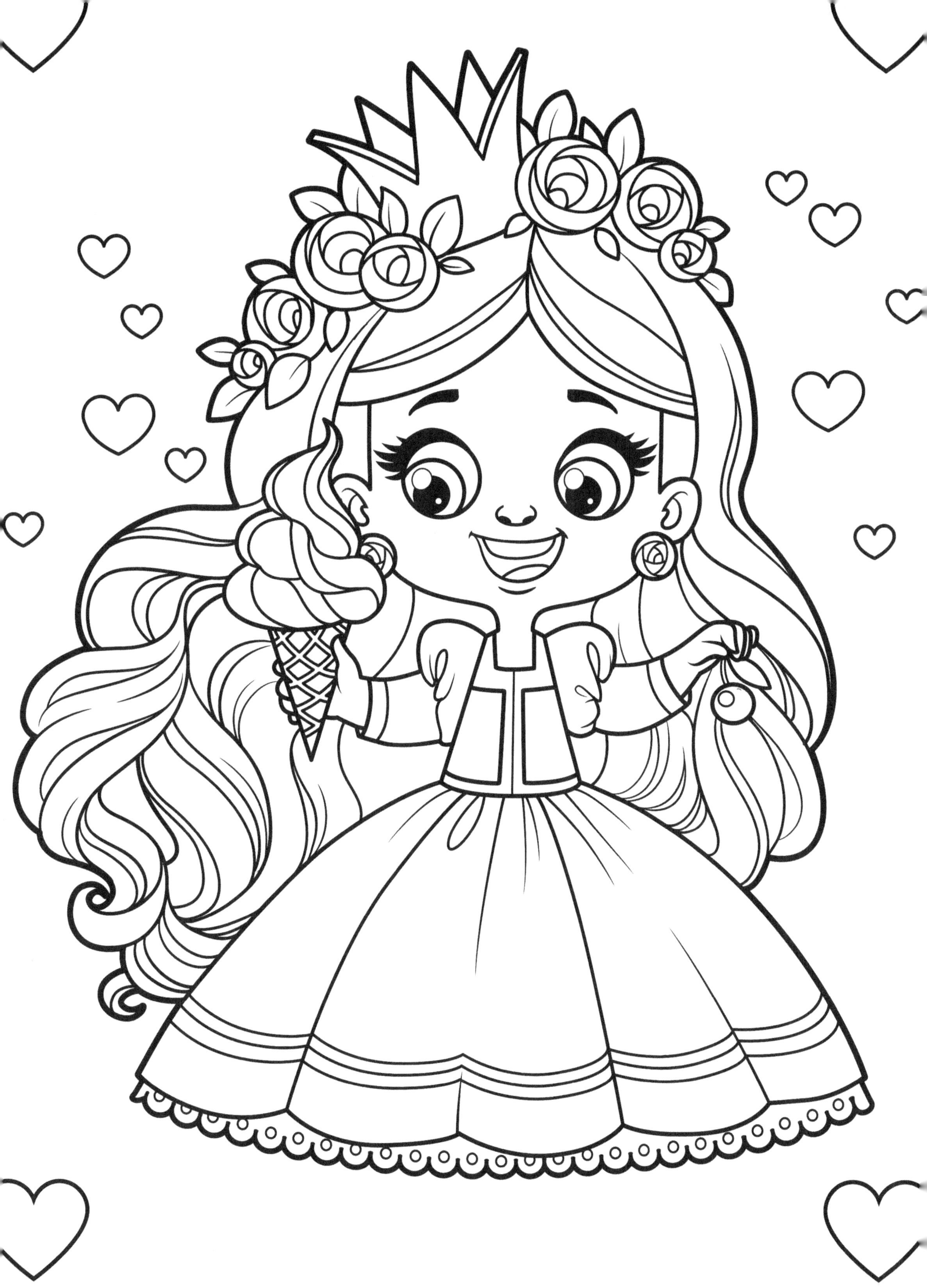

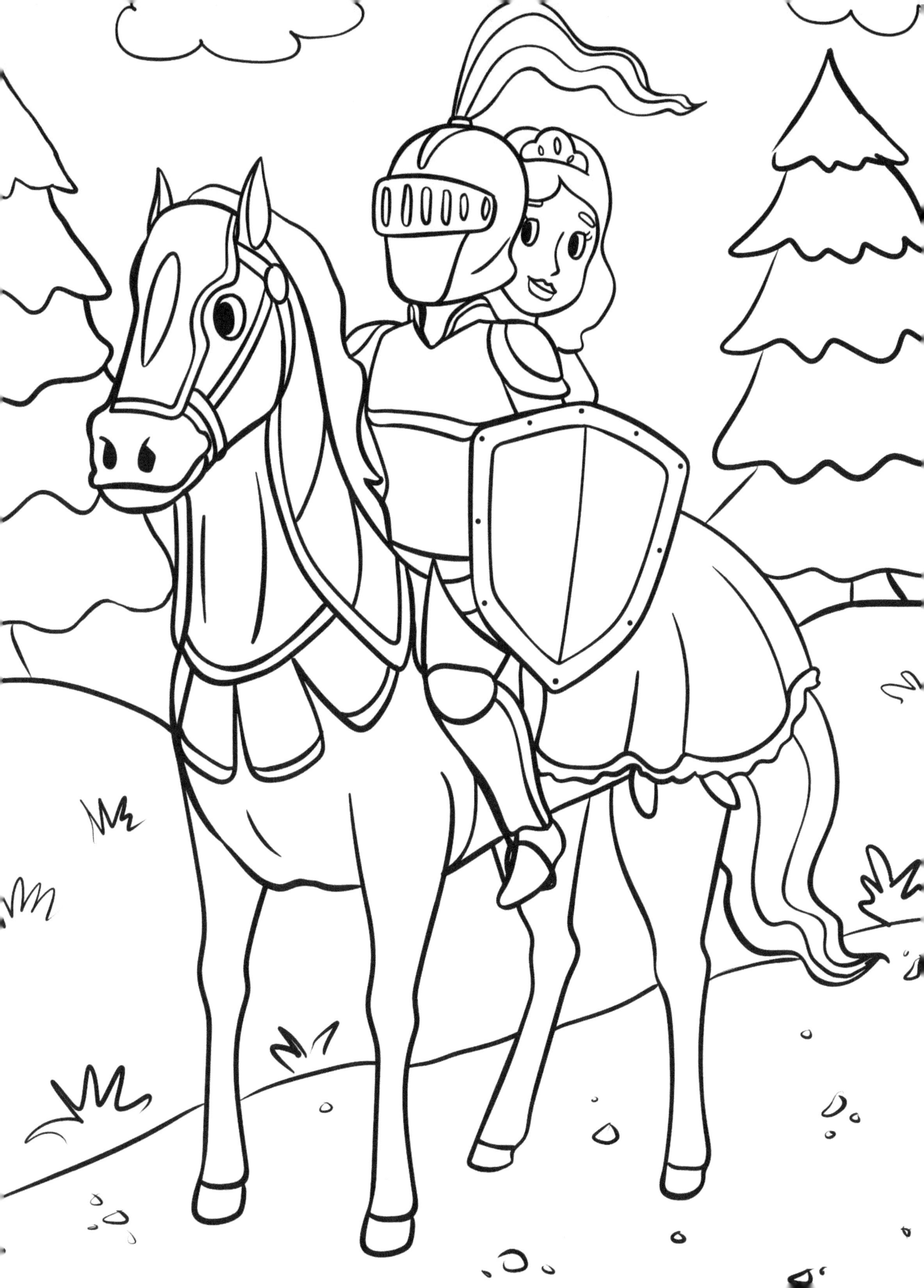

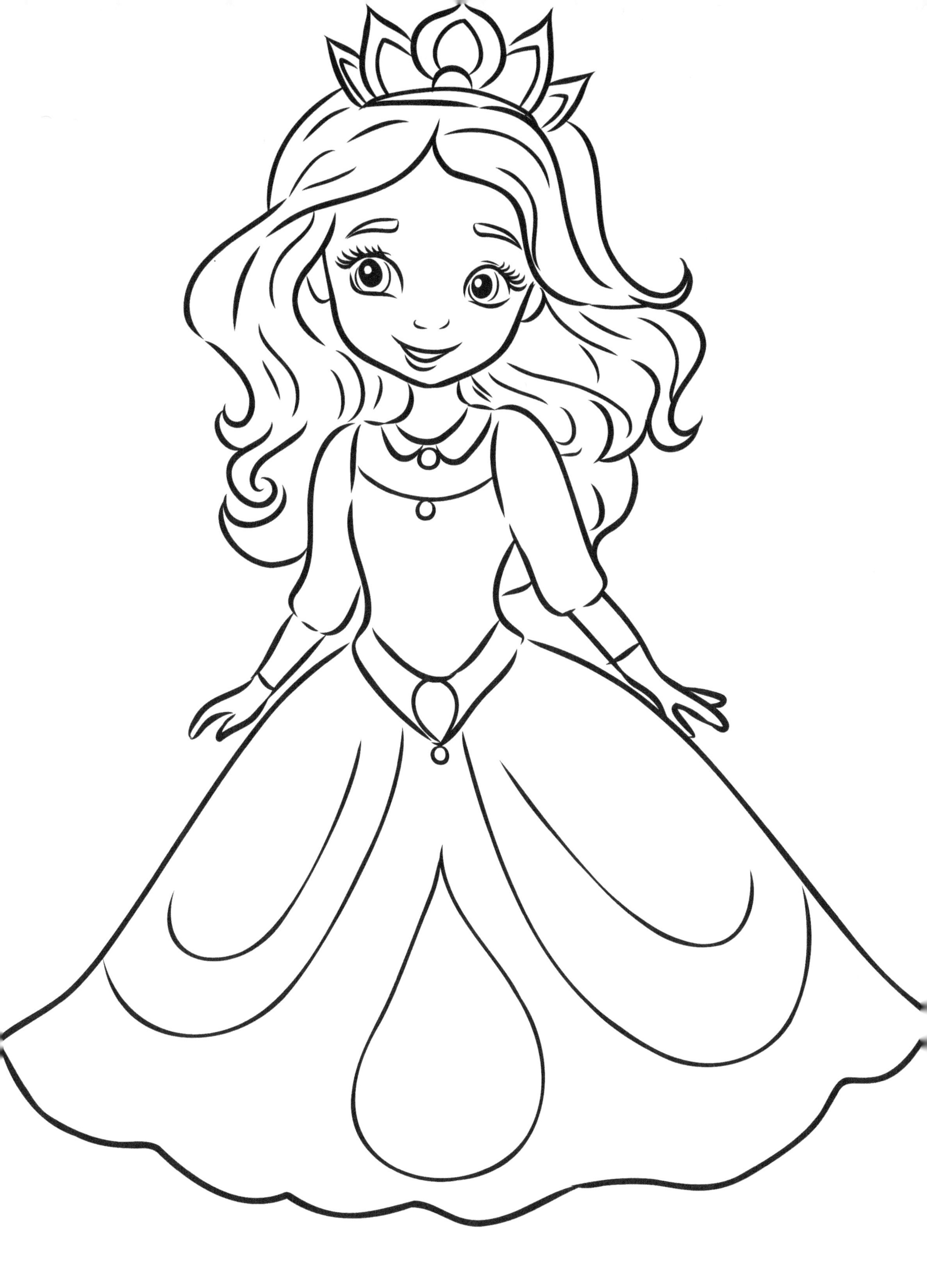

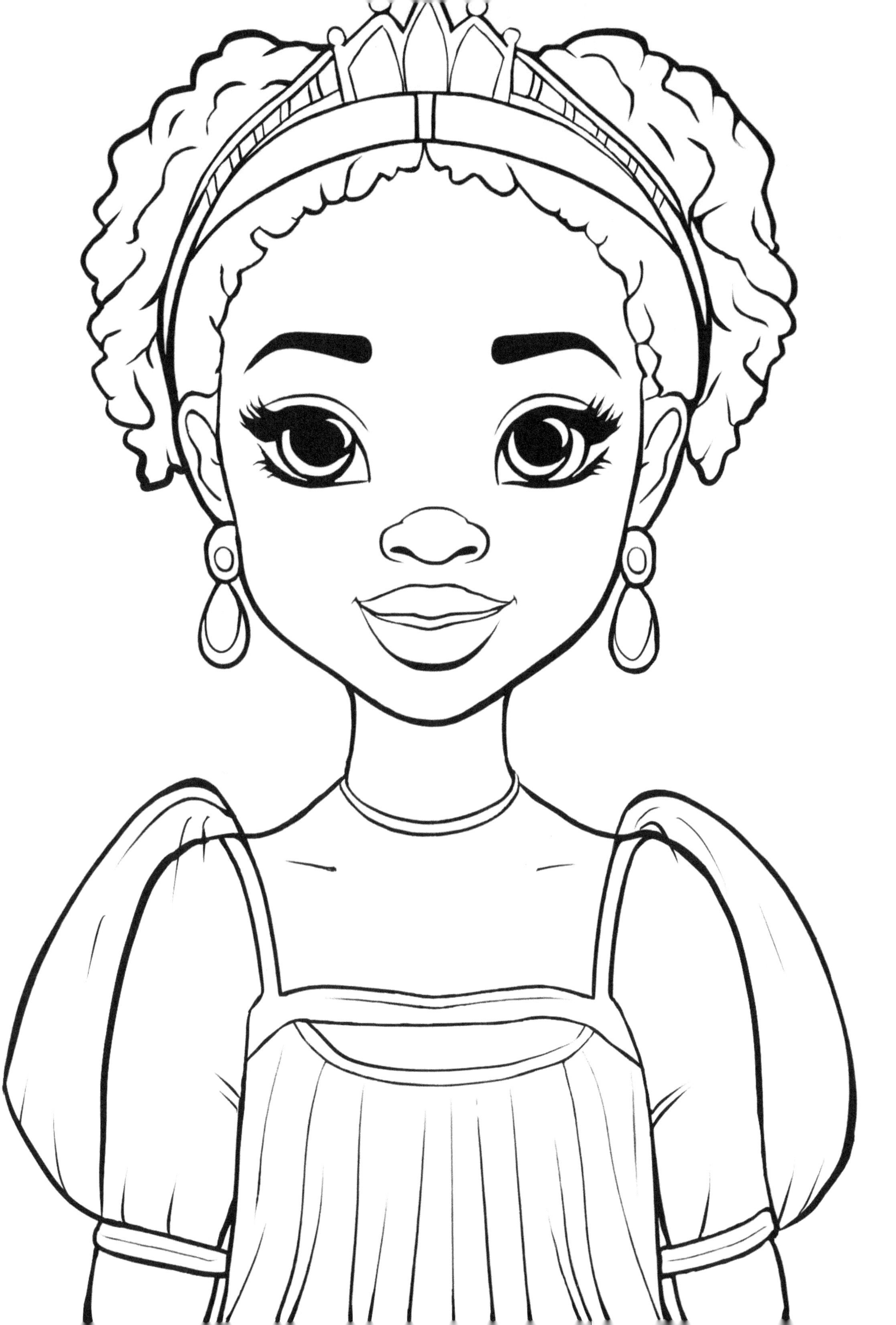

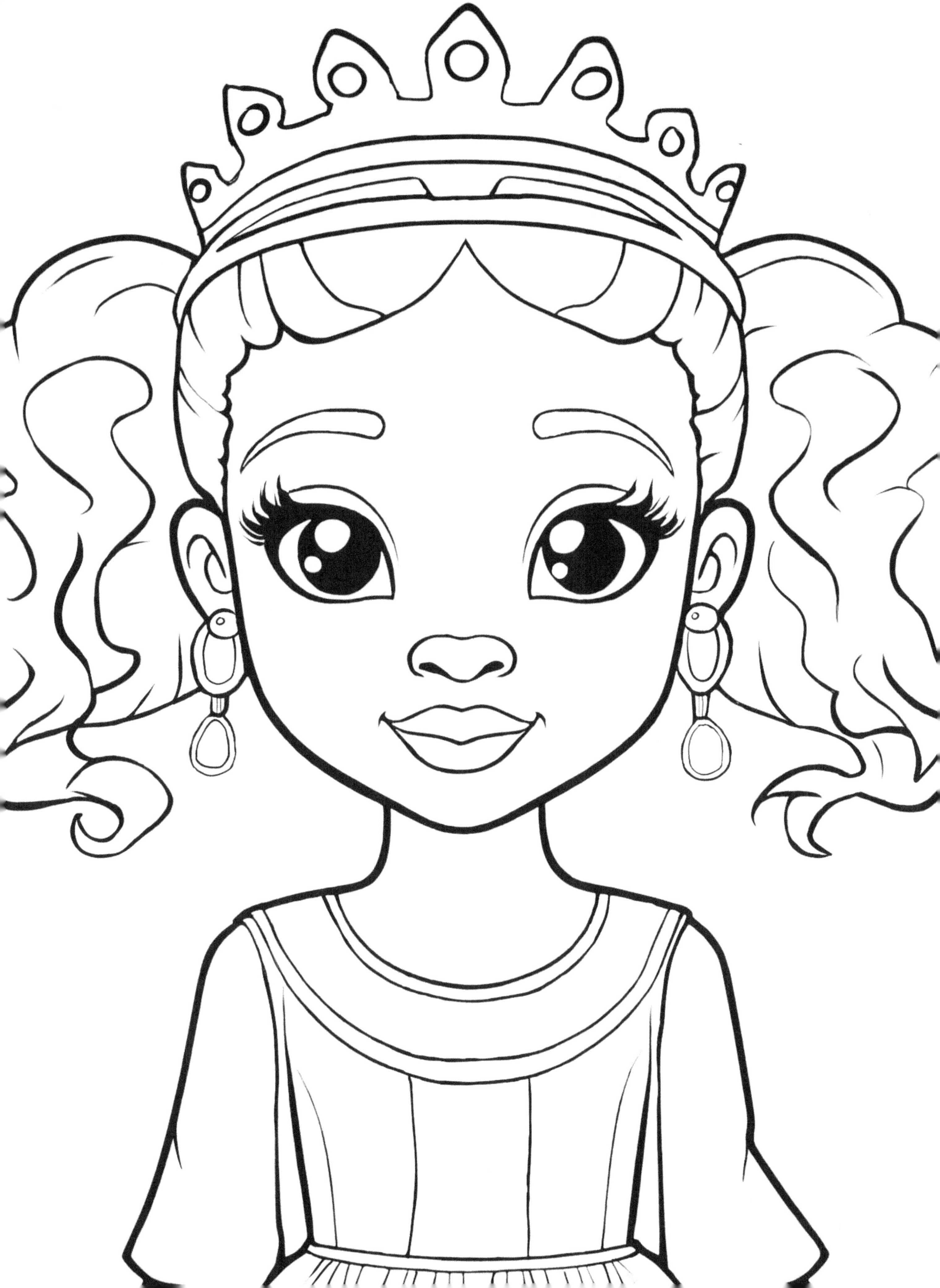

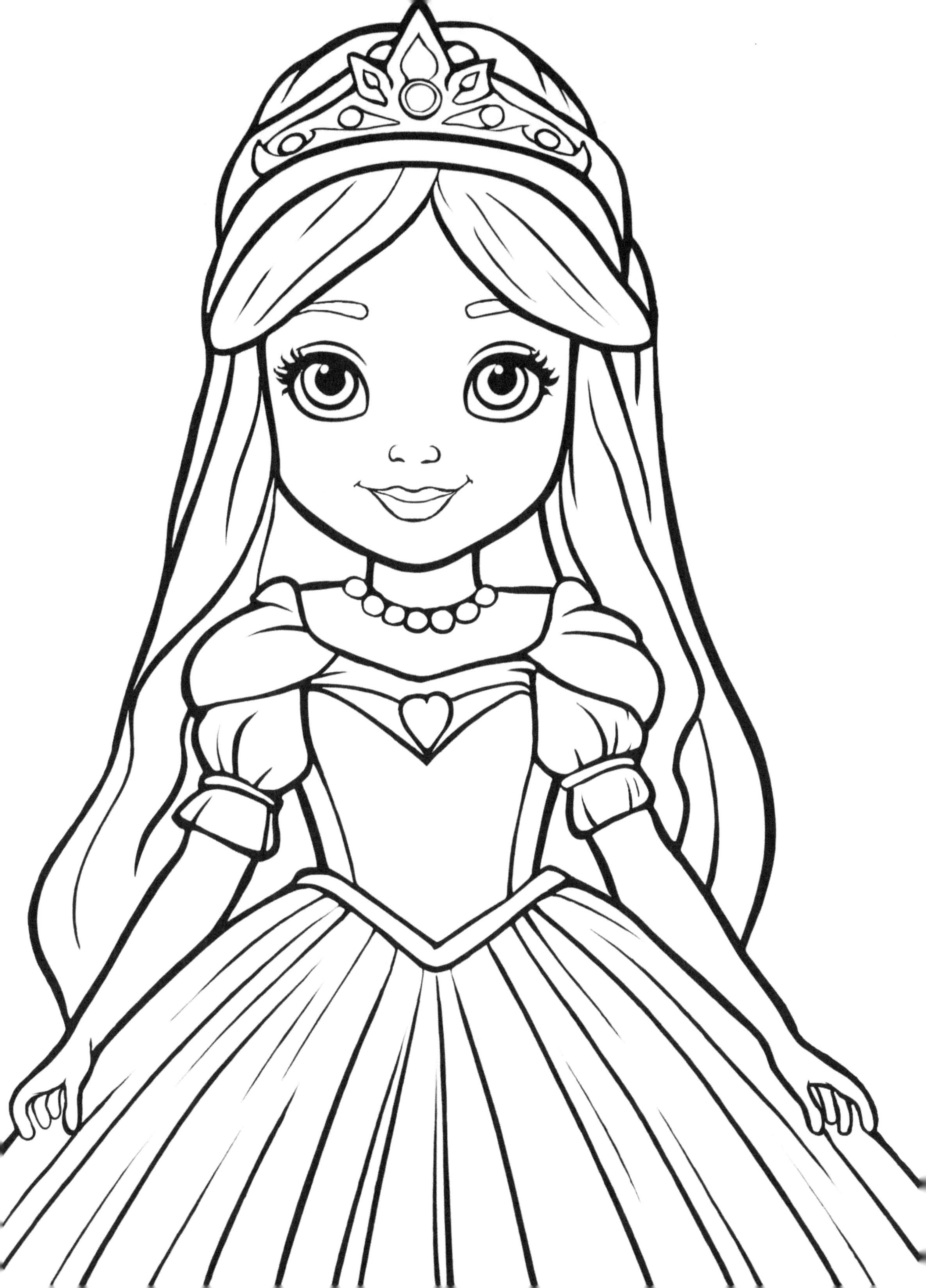

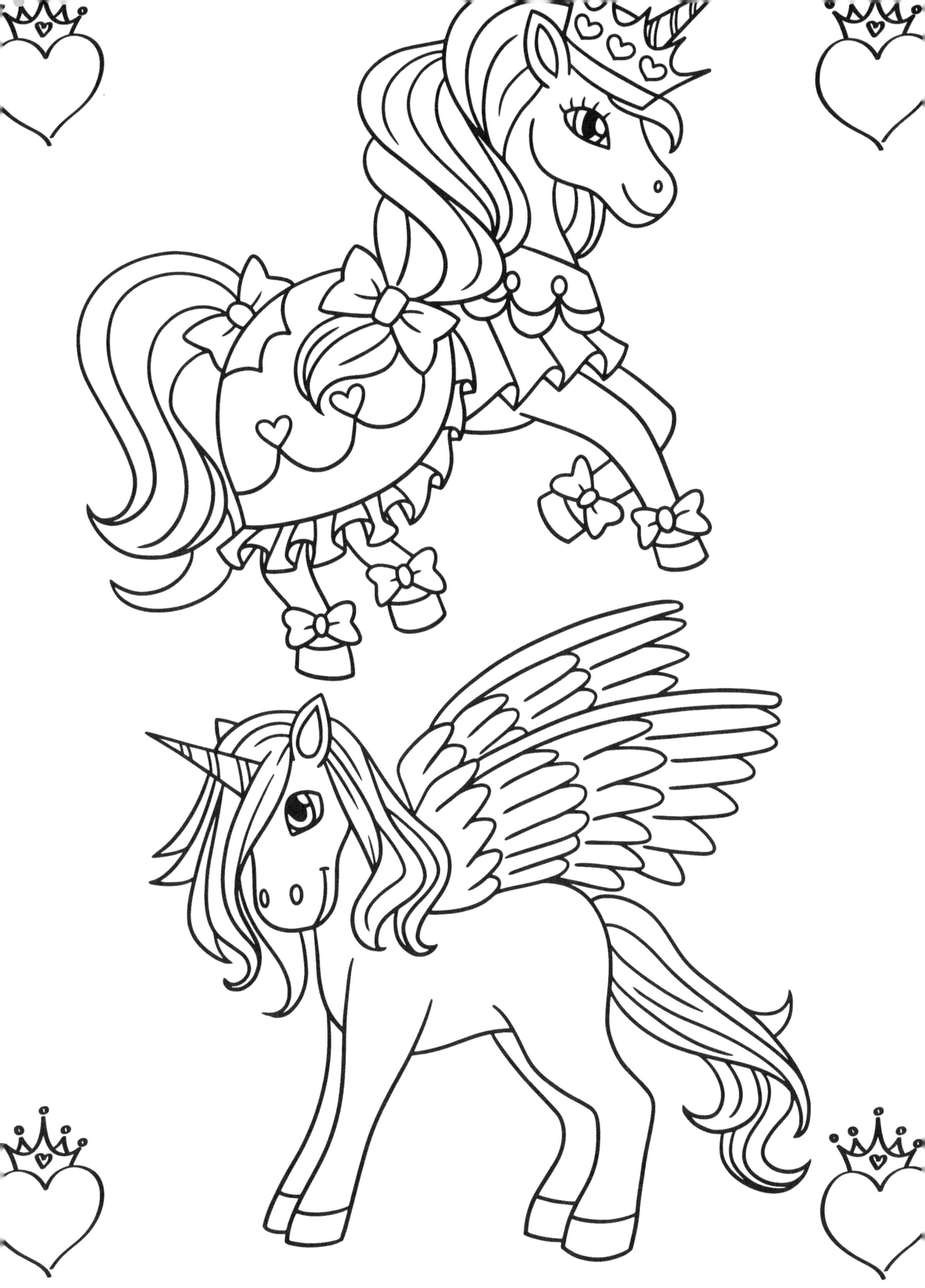

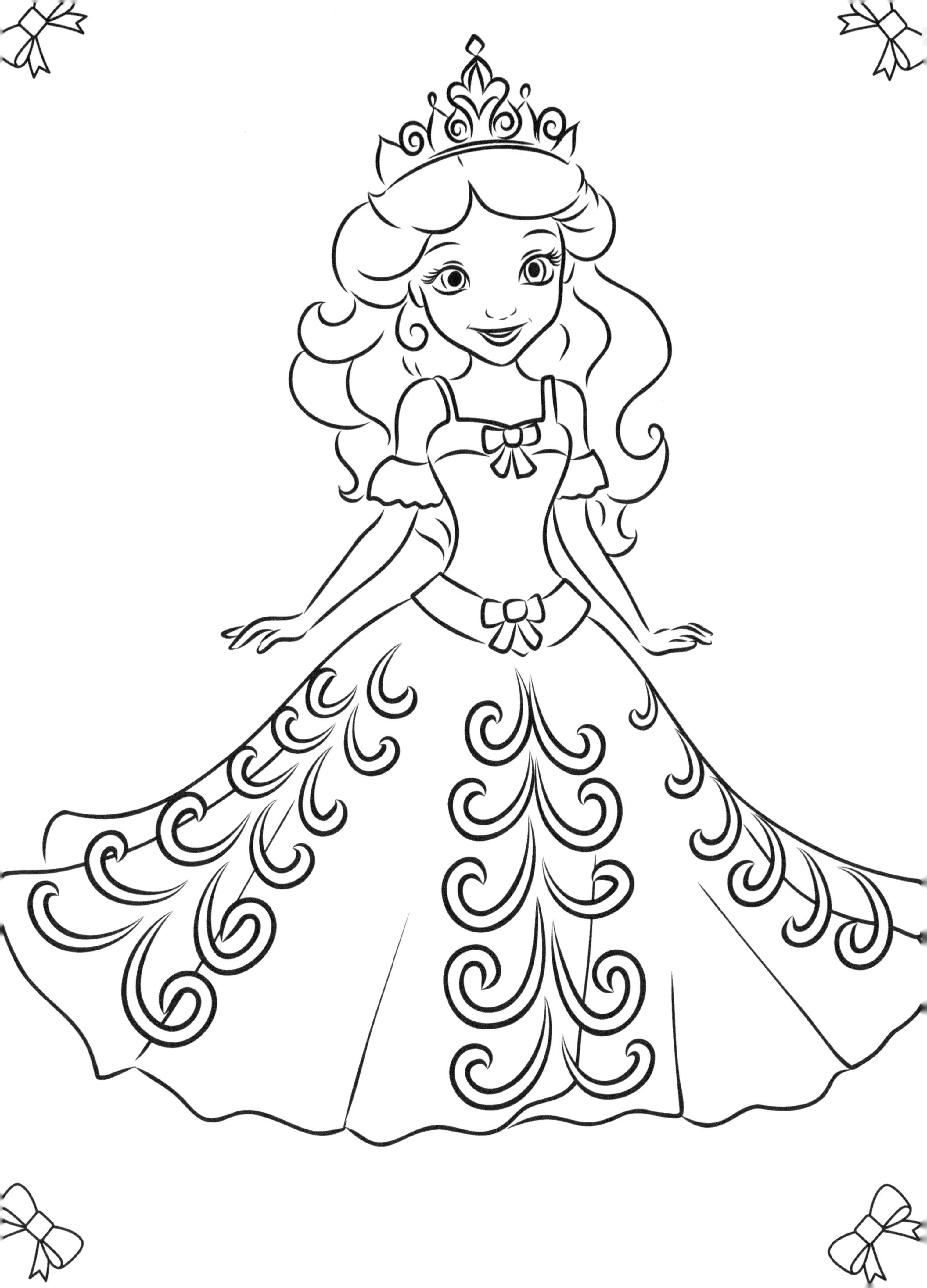

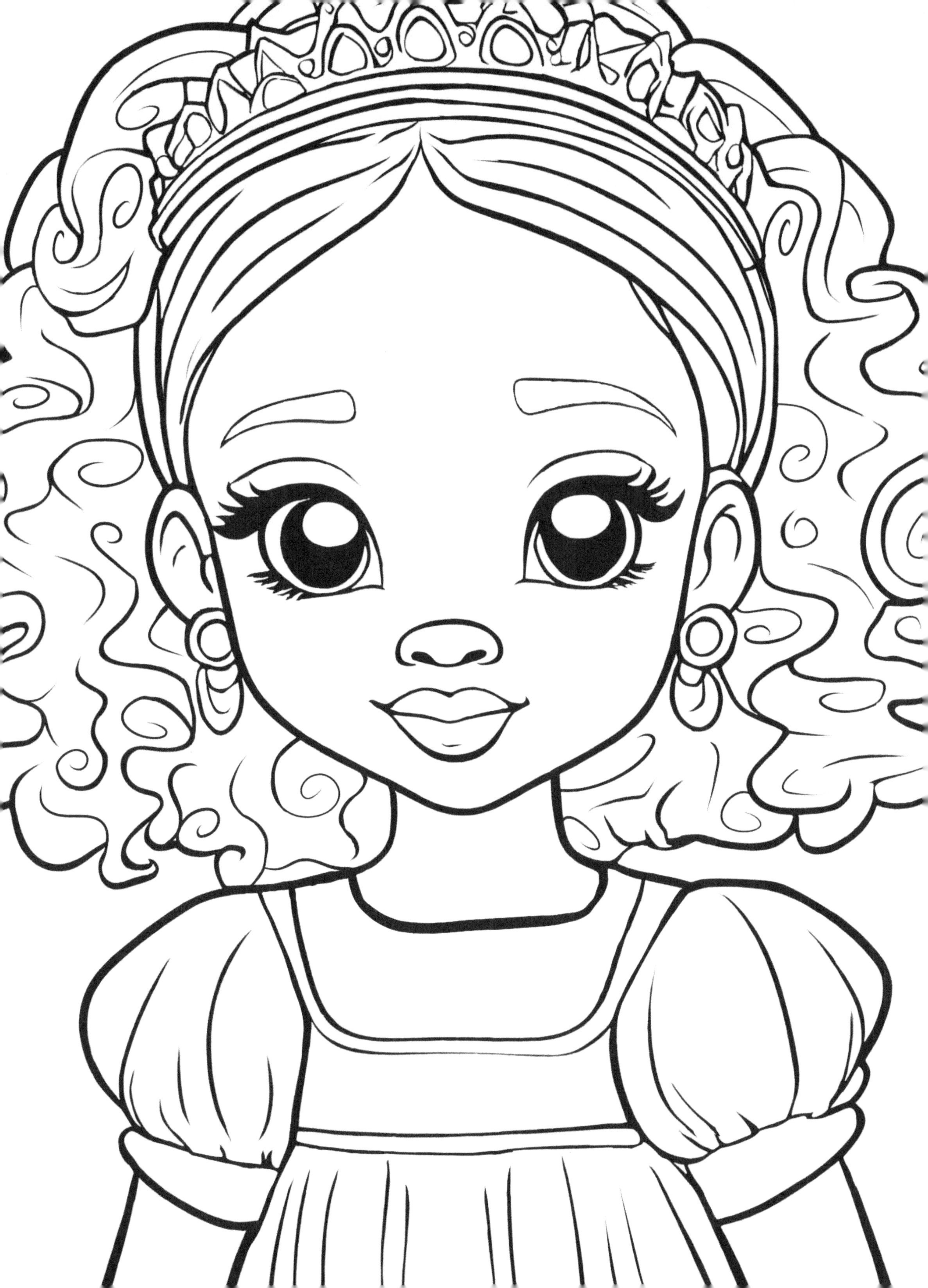

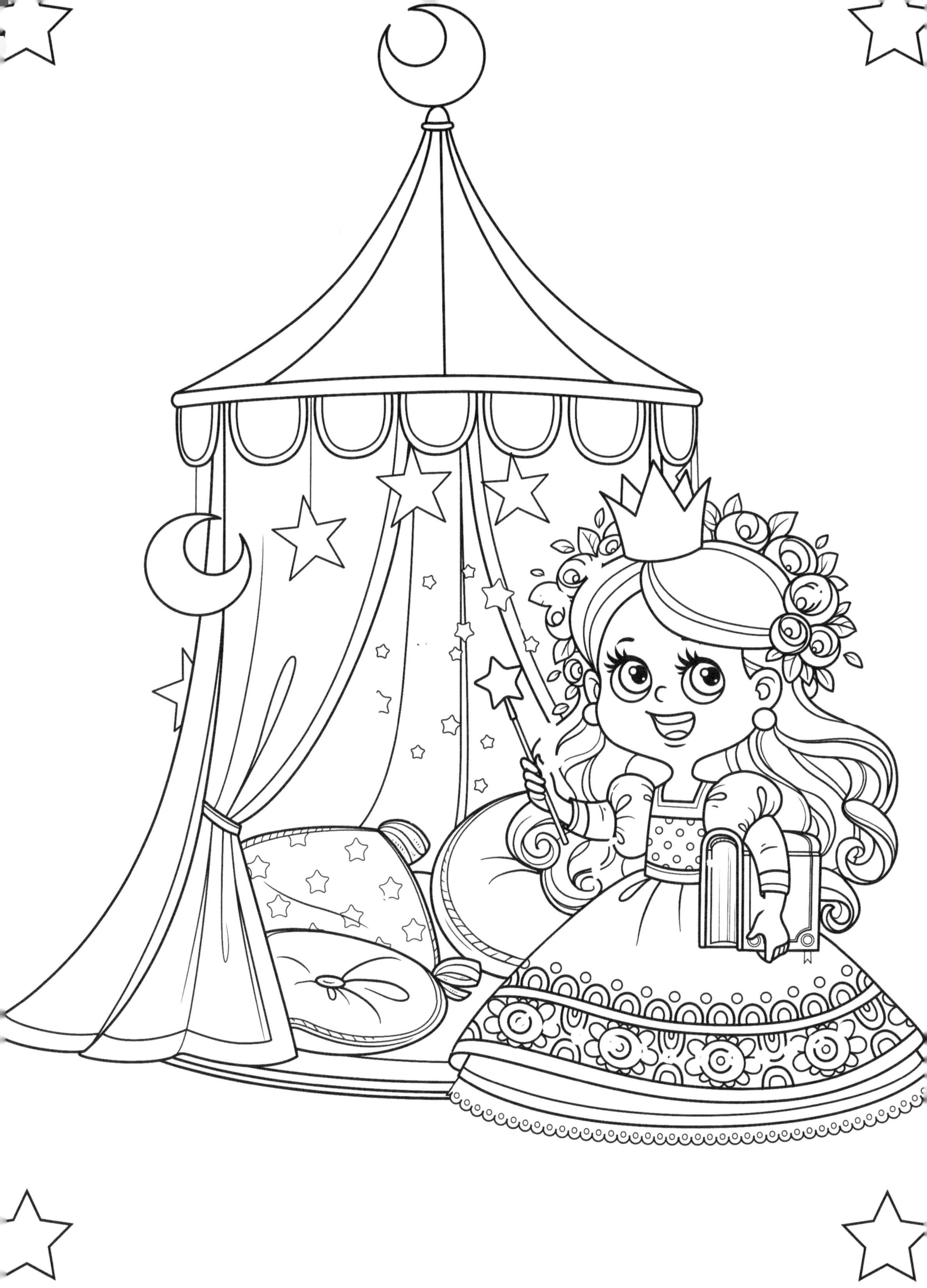

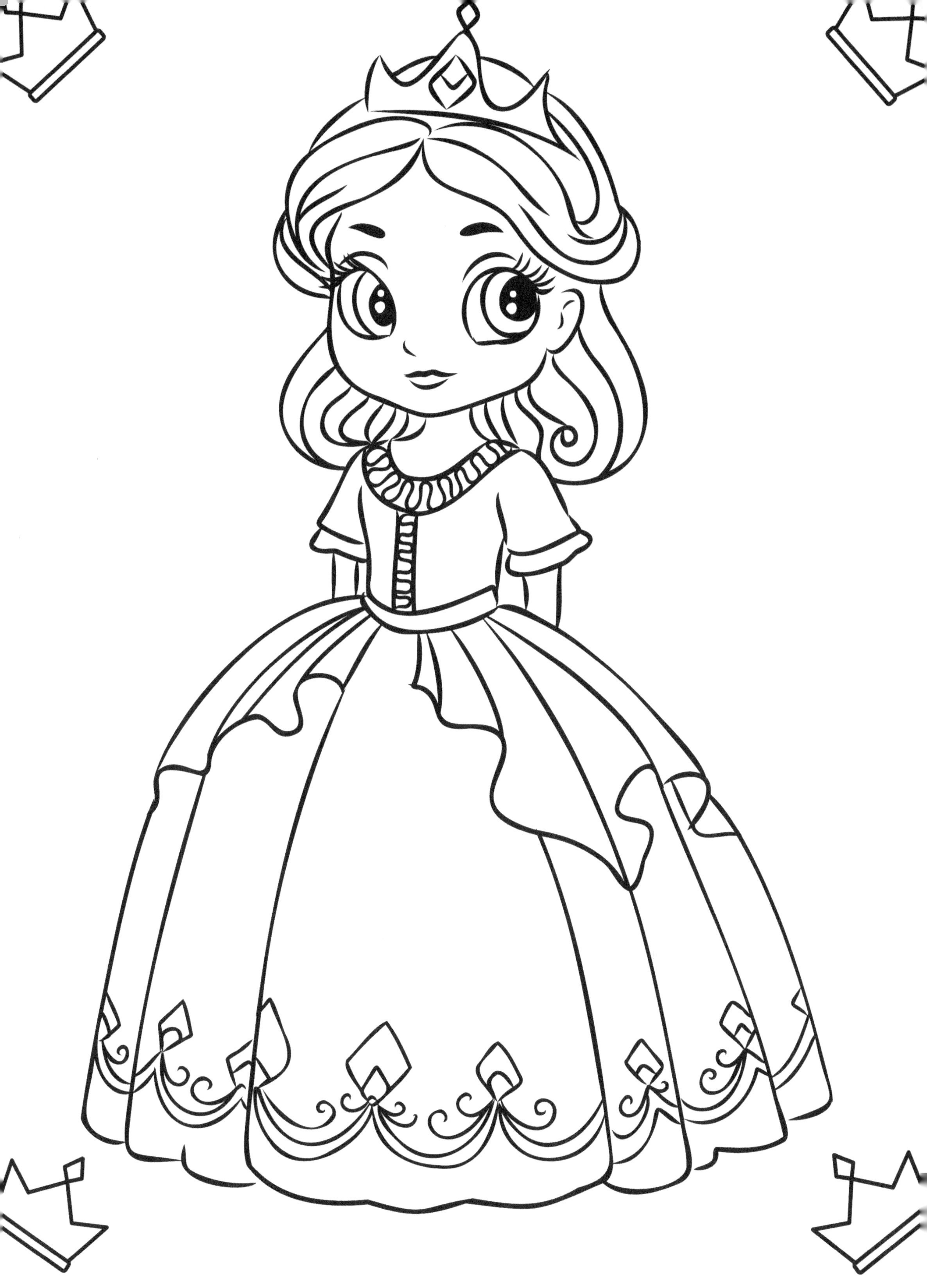

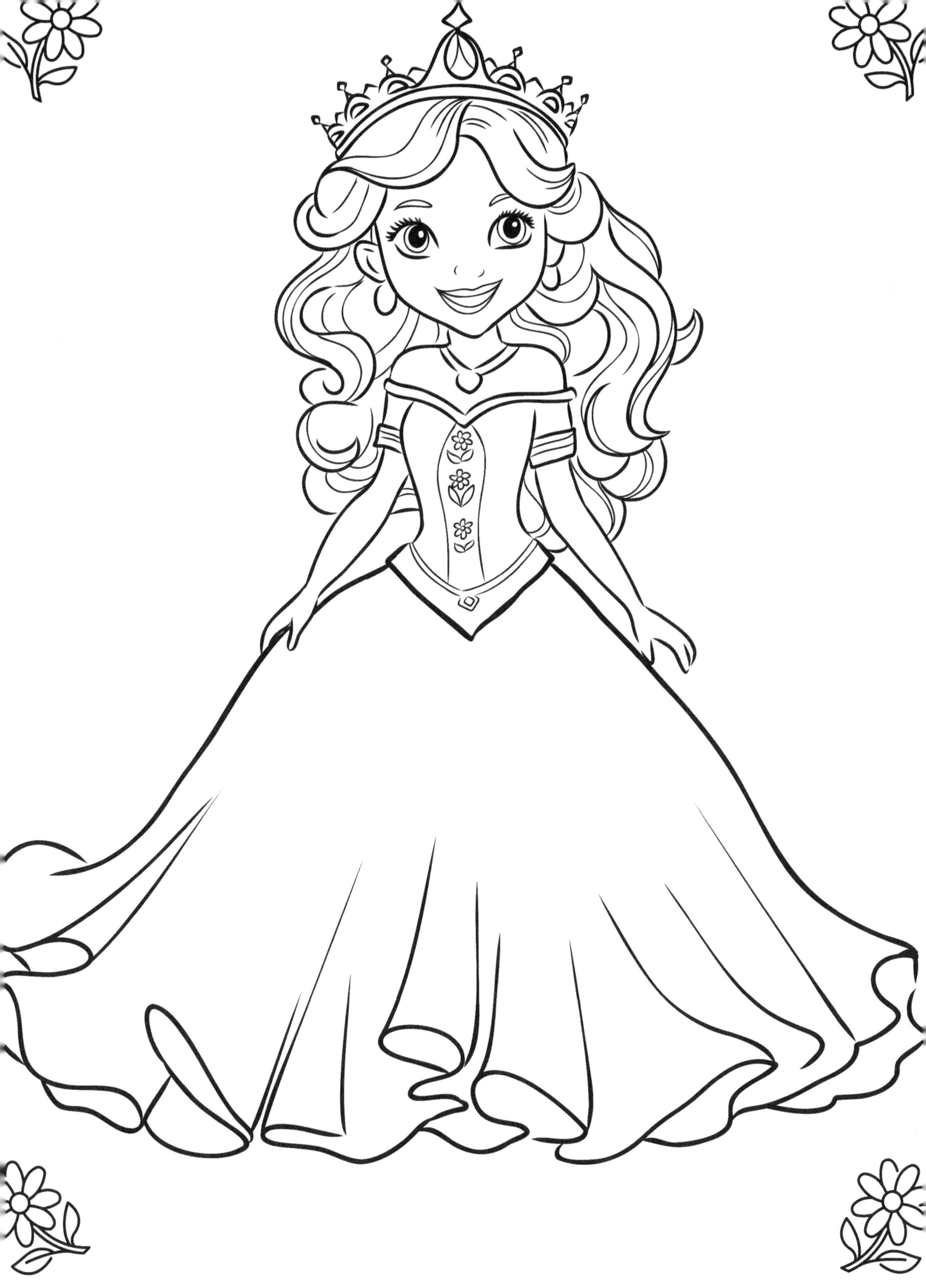

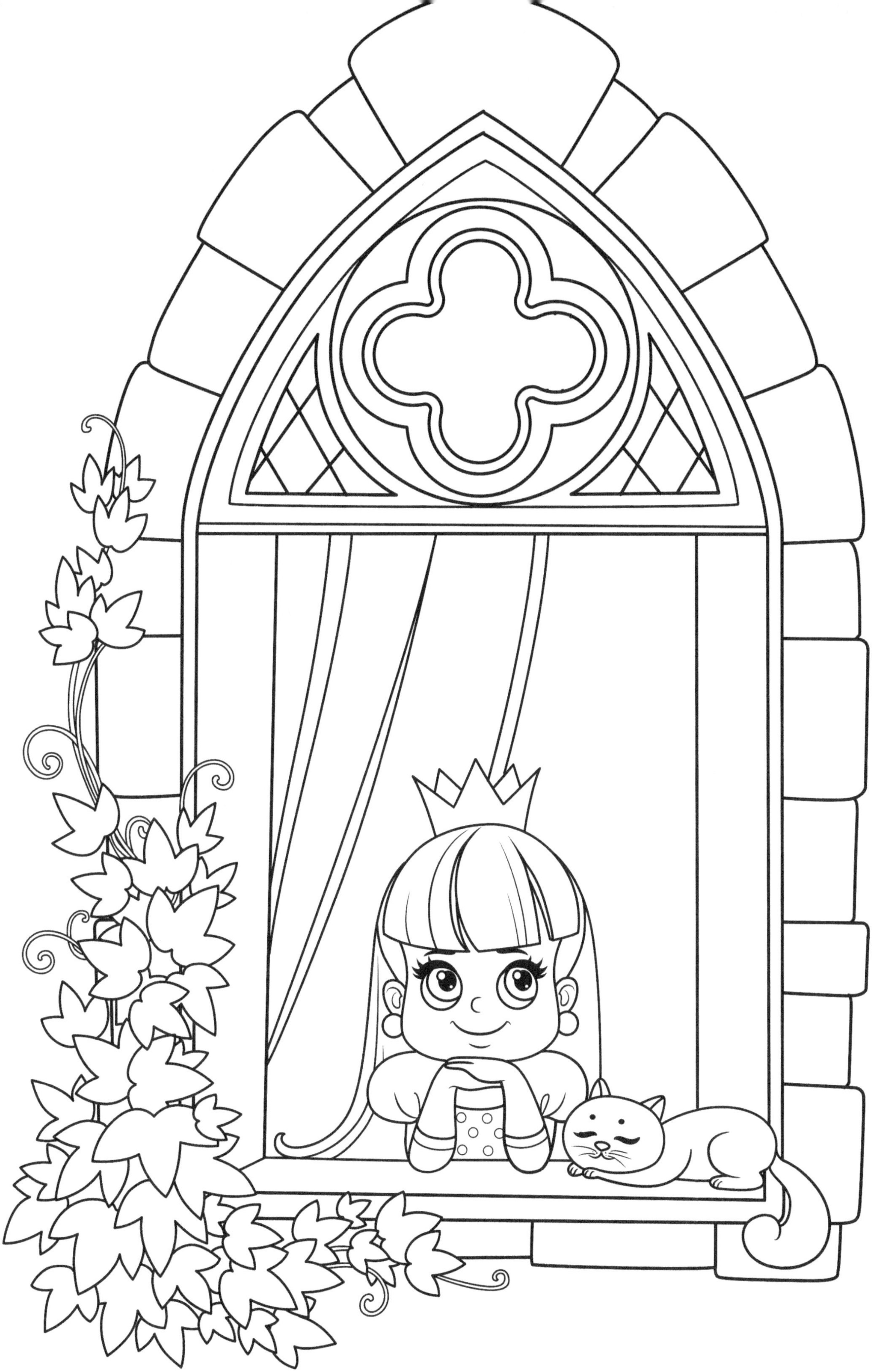

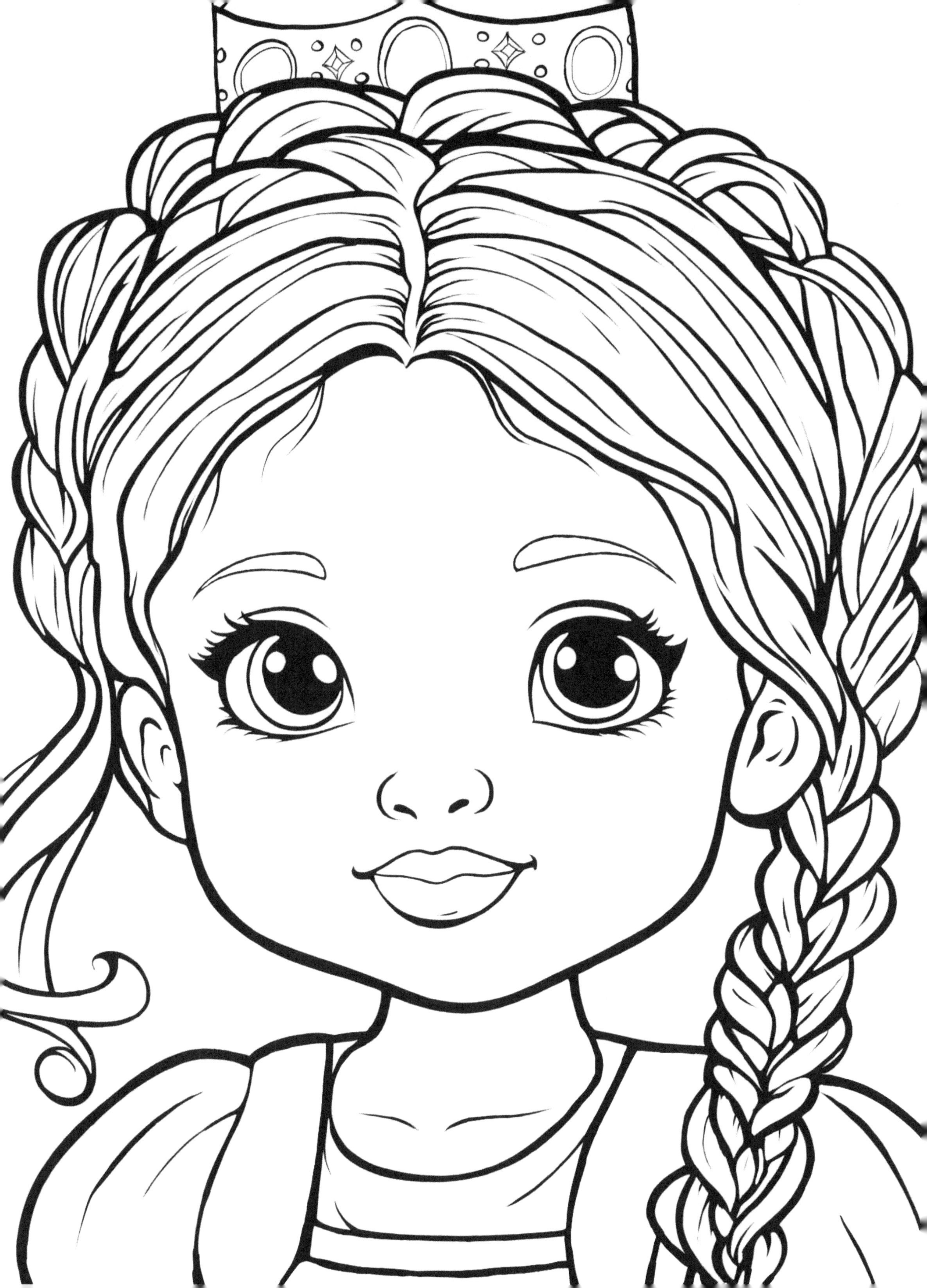

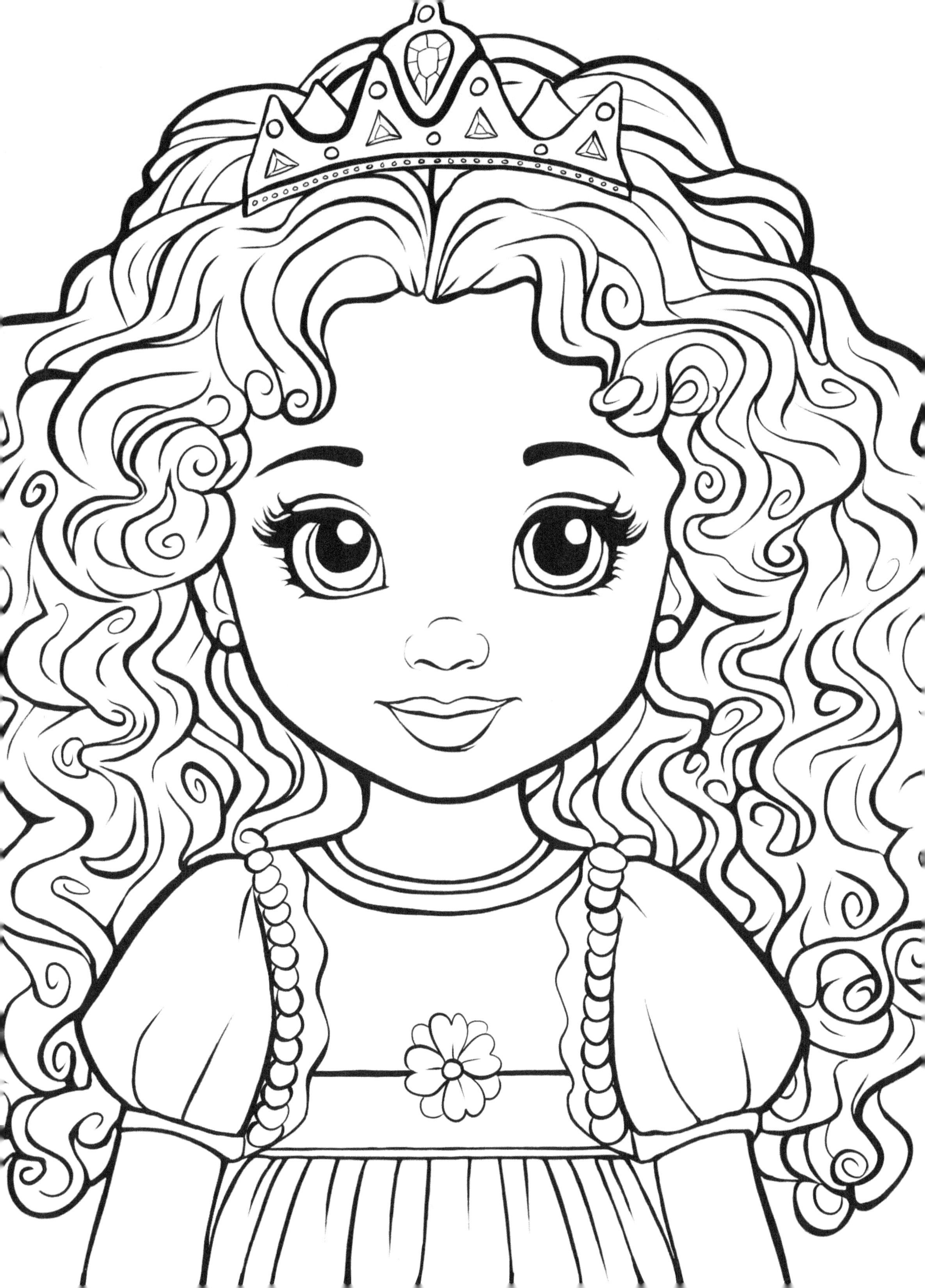

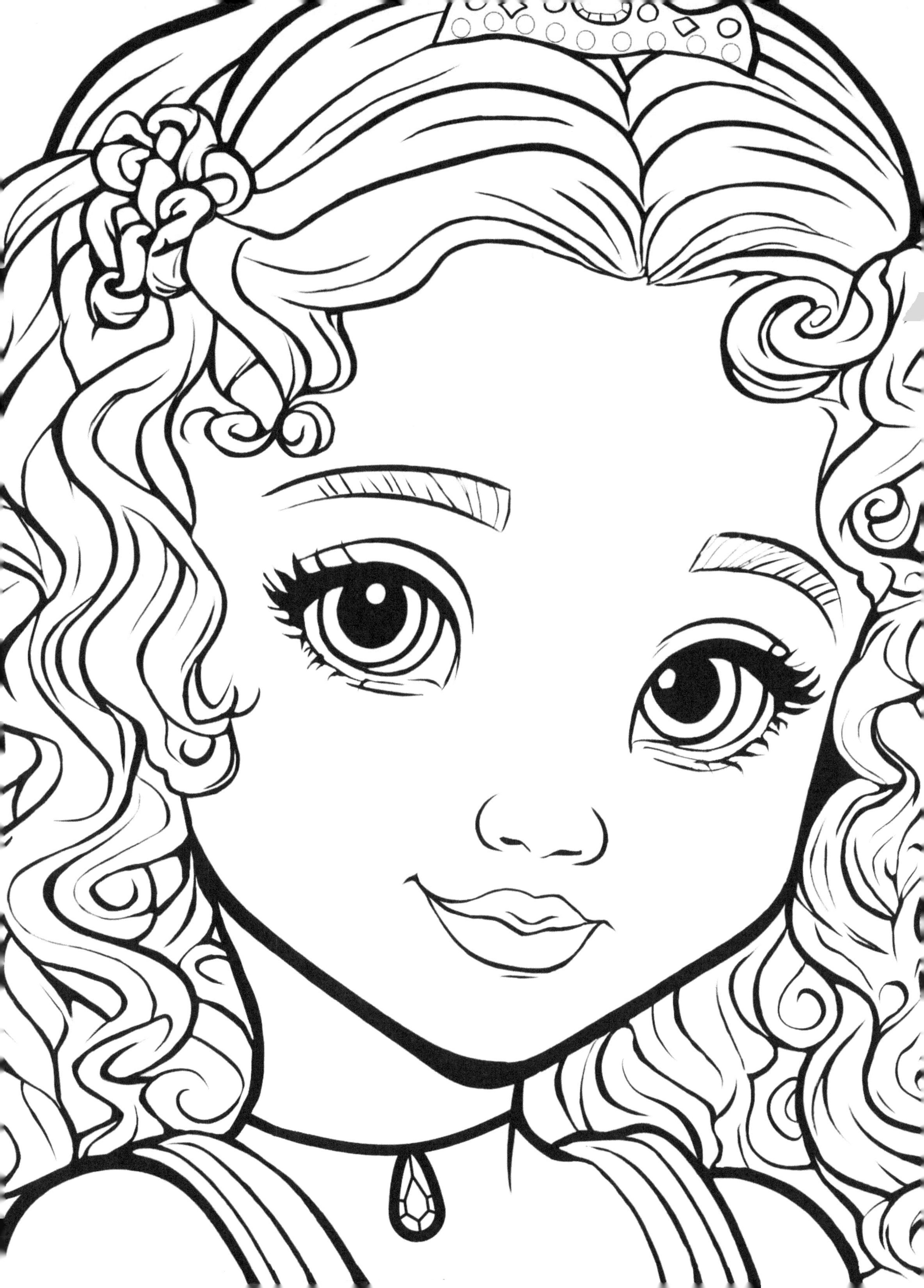

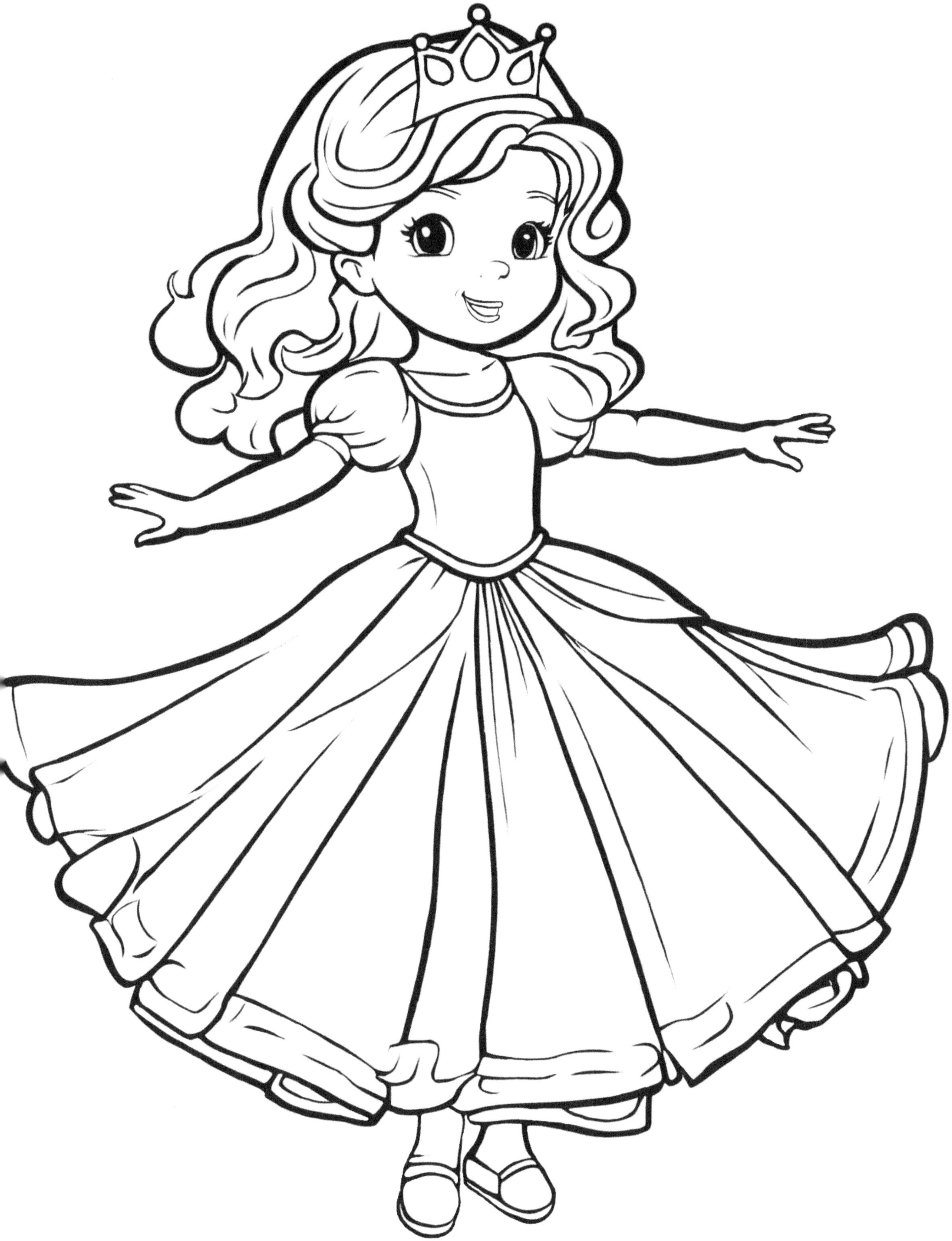

www.ingramcontent.com/pod-product-compliance
Lightning Source LLC
Chambersburg PA
CBHW081141290526
45795CB00006B/2333
* 9 7 9 8 8 8 2 6 2 8 0 2 3 *